THE ENTREPRENEUR'S GUIDE TO
THE BOOK OF FIVE RINGS

THE ENTREPRENEUR'S GUIDE TO
THE BOOK OF FIVE RINGS

DOMINIC HALE

SIRIUS

SIRIUS

This edition published in 2024 by Sirius Publishing, a division of
Arcturus Publishing Limited,
26/27 Bickels Yard, 151–153 Bermondsey Street,
London SE1 3HA

ISBN: 978-1-3988-4481-0
AD010975UK

Printed in China

CONTENTS

FOREWORD

The Essence of Musashi

Miyamoto Musashi, undefeated master swordsman and strategist, speaks through the ages to today's entrepreneurs with *The Book of Five Rings*, understood to have been written in 1643, two years before his death at the age of 61.

Originally intended as a martial arts manifesto, the five 'rings' refer to the five elements of fighting strategy, expressed as earth (or 'ground'), water, fire, wind and the void. The book speaks to the accumulated experience and wisdom of Musashi's impressive life, its enduring appeal a profound testament to his existence.

The author's seemingly authoritarian tone is just the natural writing style that was the order of his day. There are no prose subtleties here, but if one looks behind the commands and prescribed wisdom, what one notes is a primordial

rejection of the ego and an innate understanding that life is the journey not the destination.

The humility that infuses *The Book of Five Rings* is of paramount importance for today's entrepreneur, whether builder, opportunist, specialist or innovator.

We learn from Musashi that success is most likely to come to those who remain rooted and that one's senses must be tuned in to what is actually going on, rather than to what may or may not happen, or how one would like things to be. Sounding out the white noise of life and focusing on ourselves rather than benchmarking against others is no mean feat, and to do so requires commitment, patience, persistence and sacrifice, Musashi tells us.

He asks us to avoid anything superfluous – including earthly pleasures – to fulfil our potential. In what is perhaps the most famous quote from *The Book of Five Rings*, Musashi implores us to, 'do nothing which is of no use'.

So, while Musashi comes across as somewhat puritanical to the average contemporary citizen, his self-assuredness and absolute conviction in the efficacy of his approach is why his writings continue to resonate.

For today's Nietzschean supermen wannabes, Musashi's inference that you create your own values determined by your actions would appear to be manna from heaven. But whereas Nietzsche's writings smack of sociopathy, Musashi asks that we take responsibility for ourselves and our actions, believing it is imperative we first own our journey, our jealousies and procrastinations in order to move beyond them and become a

better person. According to him, this voyage of self-discovery will inevitably lead to enhanced resilience and self-reliance.

And as it was for Musashi, so it is for today's entrepreneur. Only by clearing the mind of petty preoccupations and moving away from the overwhelming human tendency to apportion blame for one's own inadequacies can the entrepreneur occupy the clear-headed territory necessary to grow and succeed.

At the same time, Musashi tells us we must be fearless and accept the inevitability of death. Easier said than done, of course, since it is one of the fundamental existential conundrums all humans seek to solve. But, deep down, we know, as Musashi knew, that only once we stop worrying about dying can we truly start living.

Background

Born in 1584 in an impoverished Japan marked by conflict, Miyamoto Musashi flourished as an adult thanks to the order imposed by Tokugawa Ieyasu, who became shogun in 1600 and began a virtual dynasty that held sway until the Imperial Restoration of 1868. Shoguns were warlords who held power alongside the emperor. As military leaders their influence, especially from the time of Ieyasu onwards, superseded that of the emperor, who functioned more as a spiritual or ceremonial figure. Ieyasu bound the country's previously troublesome lords to him through material favour, and deployed a network of spies to inform him of unrest and dissent. To emphasize his separateness and independence

from Japan's titular ruler, Ieyasu set up his power base at Edo (later renamed Tokyo), though he was careful to pay the requisite taxes and tributes that by tradition were due to the emperor in the capital at Kyoto.

In consolidating his power in this way, Ieyasu and his successors as shogun were able to exercise near total control over every aspect of people's lives. In doing so, they established a social hierarchy that ran in descending order from samurai, to farmer, artisan and merchant.

Musashi belonged to the elite samurai class, which remained synonymous with the old traditions; in particular, the sword art of Kenjutsu, which translates as the 'art' or 'science' of the sword. Musashi devoted himself to mastering this traditional form of sword fighting, and it became the guiding light in his quest for enlightenment. Such was his commitment to preserving the way of the samurai, Musashi – as all the best entrepreneurs do – broke the mould by conceiving not one but two new sword techniques, known collectively as Niten Ichi-ryū, loosely translated as 'two heavens as one'.

In the way he approached life and conducted himself, Musashi sought to exemplify the core Bushidō ('way of the warrior') principles of samurai culture, such as honour, loyalty and frugality. More than that, he strove to build on existing interpretations of them. This is something that informs Japan's unique business culture to this day. The warrior spirit of Bushidō is still invoked to inspire employees to work hard, excel and display loyalty as a mark of their personal honour.

Outside Japan, invoking the ideals of Bushidō may be a harder sell for today's entrepreneurs looking to get the best from those they rely on, but the code's emphasis on promoting trust, respect and harmony are sound foundations for success for those who care to look. Musashi's call to act honourably, aim high and become a team player is perhaps even more appropriate in today's sometimes faithless commercial realm than it was in seventeenth-century Japan, where existing and well-established notions of duty, obligation and responsibility already served to regulate social relationships.

Offering up a code of honour alongside enhanced swordsmanship, Musashi's embracing of Kenjutsu made suppressing the ego that much easier. So physically and mentally taxing was the practice that Musashi came to realize that 'letting go' was the only route available to a plane previously curtained off to him by the usual human efforts he was deploying to control and dominate his own impulses. This brought with it the capacity to see no distinction between life and death, meaning he was able to access a true state of fearlessness. In doing so, he freed a huge part of his headspace to focus on the matters at hand – namely, becoming the best swordsman he could be. This gave him a huge advantage over his contemporaries, to which his perfect record of 61 undefeated duelling contests as a swordsman pays testament.

Entrepreneurs take note – the best, the only way to alleviate existential concerns regarding the success or otherwise of that which you seek to do is to stop fretting about all the hypothetical calamities that could come to pass and focus

instead on creating the optimum conditions for success. Today, we call this 'mindfulness' or 'being present'.

Kenjutsu, which evolved into the modern martial art of Kendo, was synonymous with focus, self-discipline and restraint – essential attributes for any entrepreneur. It came with a non-negotiable code of honour that its samurai practitioners had to adhere to where the ever-present prospect of death was woven into the fabric of everyday life. Musashi's all-embracing dedication to Kenjutsu created fertile conditions within him for personal growth, allowing him to discern opportunity where others saw unsanctionable risk.

Avoid the cycle of repeat

For Musashi, the only way to develop adaptability, which he deemed of crucial importance, was to embrace the concept of uncertainty. And so it is for the modern entrepreneur, who must be able to pivot in response to any new or surprising situation. This contrasts with the endless predictive modelling that many are prone to as part of forlorn efforts to exercise mastery and control. Only when one stops seeking what is unknowable can the journey of self-improvement begin.

By developing a Musashi-style growth mindset, entre-preneurs will see their stress levels plummet and burn-out kept at bay. What's more, in giving up the impossible and exhausting quest for perfection that has knowledge of infinite permutations as a minimum requirement, time is gifted back to redirect focus to the things that count.

Many believe that hard work will, by definition, be rewarded. But if one is not working smart, those endless hours of energy expended will have been for naught. It is what one does with the time available that leads to enhanced creativity and productivity.

Why are some folk successful and others not? The answer lies in how different people apply themselves. It would be incorrect to attach to Musashi that he promoted the concept of being upwardly mobile, given he lived in a rigid society within which moving out of one's class was unthinkable. The actionable message here is that we are all capable of self-improvement – and that if you're on repeat, success is sure to elude you.

John D. Rockefeller, the US business magnate and philanthropist understood this when he said, 'if you want to succeed you should strike out on new paths, rather than travel the worn paths of accepted success'.

The world is still not a level playing field, but, extrapolating from Musashi's writings, we see that even those who've been dealt a poor hand can prosper. In other words, if you're entrepreneurially minded, there is nothing stopping you but yourself.

When we stop trying to be someone we're not, we communicate authentically, which is a prerequisite to building trust. And being trusted and believed is essential when it comes to securing backing – financial or otherwise.

The Five Rings

'Ground' – the first book – is that which governs the other four, and in it we find an overview of Musashi's philosophy, encompassing the building blocks of combat, the essence of strategy, and a promotion of the importance of perception. It is an opener that sets the scene and espouses the merits of substance over style, reminding us there are no short cuts. Today's entrepreneur would be wise to pay heed to Musashi's advocacy of lifelong learning and constant practice, so they may be able to respond appropriately to whichever curveball may come their way, always selecting the right tools for the job.

Book two – 'Water' – asks us to see strategy as adaptable and fluid to ensure balance and equilibrium in respect of any given situation. At the same time, it is essential to be sensitive to the big picture, while being alert to the small signs that point to a larger development.

Book three – 'Fire' – speaks of tactics and techniques, of timing, distance and different weaponry. It reminds us not to keep doing the same thing if it is not working, of the need to sometimes mix things up by wrongfooting the enemy and doing the unexpected to achieve one's goals.

'Wind' comes in at book number four and is concerned with the spiritual and psychological side of combat. It upholds the virtues of preparedness, of being intuitive, of knowing the enemy completely, and explains that a strong spirit can be cultivated. We can, in fact, learn to be the best, for we are not born that way. In this way, one can acquire knowledge of

how to dictate to, determine and control the enemy, crushing their spirit so that they 'feel' defeated.

Book five – 'The Void' – completes the quintet and is occupied with that which cannot be seen or known via conventional means, but which can be understood innately through knowledge of the first four rings.

What is an Entrepreneur?

When we talk of entrepreneurs, one thinks of those endeavouring to get a start-up off the ground. But a broader interpretation encompasses anyone with an entrepreneurial mindset, the innovators in life who identify and act on opportunity as opposed to those who come along for the ride. An entrepreneurial mindset is synonymous with resilience and adaptability, and a true entrepreneur is comfortable not having all the facts to hand. These are the people that provide the solutions that underpin socio-economic development across the globe. It would be fair to say they can also create – sometimes inadvertently – new problems requiring new solutions, the existential spectre of artificial intelligence (AI) being a much discussed example.

Musashi is famed for his critical thinking in that he analysed and evaluated the available evidence and arguments in a rational and unbiased manner to reach his conclusions and proceeded accordingly. Similarly, entrepreneurs today must harness their natural curiosity and blend it with logic, not emotion, to interpret events and strike on the right course of action. The goal is value-based solutions.

The true entrepreneur is not satisfied with a quick win only to thereafter rest on their laurels. They are in a constant state of learning. Musashi warns us not to seek to 'hasten the bloom of the flower'. Similarly, the original disruptor of the automobile industry, Henry Ford, noted that 'the short successes that can be gained in a brief time and without difficulty, are not worth much'.

Received wisdom has it that entrepreneurs assume the greatest risk with a view to reaping great rewards. But Musashi was the very opposite of a risk-taker. The lesson for entrepreneurs is to reframe what you are doing. Hope is not a plan, and blind fatalistic self-belief usually sees success continuing to elude those who believe they are the chosen one and that it is just a matter of time before the world realizes it.

The sobering truth infusing *The Book of Five Rings* is that you are not inherently special to the universe. Those who understand this recognize that to elevate oneself above the competition to secure an advantage involves giving oneself over completely to the process. Things don't just happen, and a God complex will only get the entrepreneur so far before they are found out. Self-belief is good; capacity is better.

There is also a received wisdom most entrepreneurs subscribe to that you must first have multiple failures to your name upon which to cut your commercial teeth and learn humility before you hit on success. However, Musashi's determination to get it right from the outset – and his

unblemished duelling record – indicate that he considered tasting defeat to be an unnecessary apprenticeship.

'If at first you don't succeed, try, try again' is a legitimate way to operate, and no one should be put off by early failures from which lessons can be drawn. However, it is even better to succeed straight off and continue to succeed thereafter, ever-improving along the way. Musashi would tell you that *The Book of Five Rings* is a how-to guide for doing just that. Countless others would agree.

THE BOOK OF
FIVE RINGS
PREFACE

◇◇◇◇◇◇◇◇◇◇◇◇◇◇◇◇◇◇◇◇◇◇◇◇

Original Text

I have been many years training in the Way of strategy, called Niten Ichi-ryū, and now I think I will explain it in writing for the first time.

It is now during the first ten days of the tenth month in the twentieth year of Kanei [1645]. I have climbed mountain Iwato of Higo in Kyushu to pay homage to heaven, pray to Kwannon, and kneel before Buddha. I am a warrior of Harima province, Shinmen Musashi no Kami Fujiwara no Geshin, age sixty years.

From youth, my heart has been inclined toward the Way of strategy. My first duel was when I was thirteen; I struck down a strategist of the Shinto school, one Arima Kihei. When I was sixteen, I struck down an able strategist, Tadashima Akiyama. When I was twenty-one, I went up to the capital and met all manner of strategists, never once failing to win in many contests.

After that I went from province to province, duelling with strategists of various schools, and not once failed to win even though I had as many as sixty encounters. This was between the ages of thirteen and twenty-eight or twenty-nine. When I reached thirty, I looked back on my past. The previous victories were not due to my having mastered strategy. Perhaps it was natural ability, or the order of heaven, or that other schools' strategy was inferior.

After that, I studied morning and evening, searching for the principle, and came to realize the Way of strategy when I was fifty. Since then I have lived without following any particular Way. Thus, with the virtue of strategy, I practise many arts and abilities – all things with no teacher. To write this book I did not use the law of Buddha or the teachings of Confucius, neither old war chronicles nor books on martial tactics. I take up my brush to explain the true spirit of this Ichi school as it is mirrored in the Way of heaven and Kwannon. The time is the night of the tenth day of the tenth month, at the hour of the tiger [3–5 am].

INTRODUCTION

Miyamoto Musashi kicks off proceedings with a chronicle of his life to that point and his rationale for writing *The Book of Five Rings*. While the historical accuracy or otherwise of his account is debatable, it is the essence and symbolism of his life's journey we are interested in here.

Straight away, he draws our attention to his many years of training in the two-sword technique of Niten Ichi-ryū, which he conceived and describes as the Way of strategy. It is his reason for writing, we are told. This introductory curriculum vitae also tells us where he is based, that he is sixty, a Buddhist, that he was predisposed to duelling from an early age, and that his record on that front – stretching back to his earliest encounters – is an unblemished one.

He talks of a watershed moment at 30 when he realized his successes to that point may have been down to good fortune,

unchallenging opposition, or divine will, but most certainly were not down to him 'having mastered strategy', and that he needed to up his game thenceforth.

This is an especially astute, fascinating and humble insight for a man of his time. It shows entrepreneurs today that no matter how powerful they become, or how reliable the Midas touch they may have enjoyed to date, success is never a given and one is never the finished product. Dynamics are ever-changing, and one must be willing to keep learning and reach for new heights to maximize the scope for continued competitive advantage.

Musashi speaks of having thereafter dedicated himself in unwavering fashion to his quest to unlock the secrets to success, such that ten years prior to the time of writing, he considered himself to have attained the state of being he sought. This gave him the mechanism he needed that could be applied to each area of his existence for further enlightenment without any need for external inputs.

Entrepreneurs take note: true personal development does not mean the operational harvesting and processing of ever more facts and figures, which will inevitably have limited application, but rather a mastery of the psychological and emotional functions that can be brought to bear upon any situation. This is the Way of strategy Musashi describes, which simultaneously speaks of rational judgement, sound decision-making and the ability to navigate complex dynamics, alongside the capacity to manage moods and feelings to avoid acts of impulsiveness or the showing of one's hand to the competition.

CHAPTER
ONE
THE GROUND
BOOK

Original Text

Strategy is the craft of the warrior. Commanders must enact the craft, and troopers should know this Way. There is no warrior in the world today who really understands the Way of strategy.

There are various Ways. There is the Way of salvation by the law of Buddha, the Way of Confucius governing the Way of learning, the Way of healing as a doctor, as a poet teaching the Way of Waka, tea, archery, and many arts and skills. Each man practises as he feels inclined. It is said that the warrior's is the twofold Way of pen and sword, and he should have a taste for both Ways.

Even if a man has no natural ability, he can be a warrior by sticking assiduously to both divisions of the Way. Generally speaking, the Way of the warrior is resolute acceptance of death. Although not only warriors but priests, women, peasants and lowlier folk have been known to die readily in the cause of duty or out of shame, this is

a different thing. The warrior is different in that studying the Way of strategy is based on overcoming men. Through victory gained in crossing swords with individuals, or enjoining battle with large numbers, we can attain power and fame for ourselves or for our lord. This is the virtue of strategy.

The Way of Strategy

In China and Japan, practitioners of the Way have been known as 'masters of strategy'. Warriors must learn this Way.

Recently there have been people getting on in the world as strategists, but they are usually just sword-fencers. The

attendants of the Kashima Kantori shrines of the province Hitachi received instruction from the gods, and made schools based on this teaching, travelling from country to country instructing men. This is the recent meaning of strategy.

In olden times, strategy was listed among the Ten Abilities and Seven Arts as a beneficial practice. It was certainly an art, but as beneficial practice it was not limited to sword-fencing. The true value of sword-fencing cannot be seen within the confines of sword-fencing technique.

If we look at the world, we see arts for sale. Men use equipment to sell their own selves. As if with the nut and the flower, the nut has become less than the flower. In this kind of Way of strategy, both those teaching and those learning the Way are concerned with colouring and showing off their technique, trying to hasten the bloom of the flower. They speak of 'This Dōjō' and 'That Dōjō'. They are looking for profit. Someone once said, 'Immature strategy is the cause of grief.' That was a true saying.

The Four Ways

There are four Ways in which men pass through life: as gentlemen, farmers, artisans and merchants.

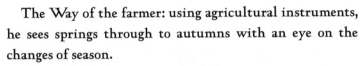

The Way of the farmer: using agricultural instruments, he sees springs through to autumns with an eye on the changes of season.

Second is the Way of the merchant. The winemaker obtains his ingredients and puts them to use to make his living. The Way of the merchant is always to live by taking profit. This is the Way of the merchant.

Thirdly the gentleman warrior, carrying the weaponry of his Way. The Way of the warrior is to master the virtue of his weapons. If a gentleman dislikes strategy he will not appreciate the benefit of weaponry, so must he not have a little taste for this?

Fourthly the Way of the artisan. The Way of the carpenter is to become proficient in the use of his tools, first to lay his plans with a true measure and then perform his work according to plan. Thus, he passes through life.

These are the Four Ways – of the gentleman, the farmer, the artisan and the merchant.

Comparing the Way of the Carpenter to Strategy

The comparison with carpentry is through the connection with houses. Houses of the nobility, houses of warriors, the Four Houses, ruin of houses, thriving of houses, the style

of the house, the tradition of the house, and the name of the house. The carpenter uses a master plan of the building, and the Way of strategy is similar in that there is a plan of campaign. If you want to learn the craft of war, ponder over this book. The teacher is as a needle, the disciple is as thread. You must practise constantly.

Like the foreman carpenter, the commander must know natural rules, and the rules of the country, and the rules of houses. This is the Way of the foreman.

The foreman carpenter must know the architectural theory of towers and temples, and the plans of palaces, and must employ men to raise up houses. The Way of the foreman carpenter is the same as the Way of the commander of a warrior house.

In the construction of houses, choice of woods is made. Straight unknotted timber of good appearance is used for the revealed pillars, straight timber with small defects is used for the inner pillars. Timber of the finest appearance, even if a little weak, is used for the thresholds, lintels, doors, and sliding doors, and so on. Good, strong timber, though it be gnarled and knotted, can always be used discreetly in construction. Timber which is weak or knotted throughout should be used as scaffolding, and later for firewood.

The foreman carpenter allots his men work according to their ability. Floor layers, makers of sliding doors, thresholds and lintels, ceilings and so on. Those of lesser ability lay the floor joists, carve wedges and do such miscellaneous work. If the foreman knows and deploys his men well, the finished work will be good. The foreman should take into account the abilities and limitations of his men, circulating among them and asking nothing unreasonable. He should know their morale and spirit, and encourage them when necessary. This is the same as the principle of strategy.

The Way of Strategy

Like a trooper, the carpenter sharpens his own tools. He carries his equipment in his tool box, and works under the direction of his foreman. He makes columns and girders with an axe, shapes floorboards and shelves with a plane, cuts fine openwork and carvings accurately, giving as excellent a finish as his skill will allow. This is the craft of the carpenter. When the carpenter grows to be skilled and understands measures, he can become a foreman.

The carpenter's attainment is, having tools which will cut well, to make small shrines, writing shelves, tables, paper lanterns, chopping boards and pot-lids. These are

the specialities of the carpenter. Things are similar for the trooper. You ought to think deeply about this.

The attainment of the carpenter is that his work is not warped, that the joints are not misaligned, and that the work is truly planed so that it meets well and is not merely finished in sections. This is essential. If you want to learn this Way, deeply consider the things written in this book one at a time. You must do sufficient research.

Outline of the Five Books of this Book of Strategy

The Way is shown in five books concerning different aspects. These are Ground, Water, Fire, Tradition [Wind], and Void.

The body of the Way of strategy from the viewpoint of my Ichi school is explained in the Ground Book. It is difficult to realize the true Way just through sword-fencing. Know the smallest things and the biggest things, the shallowest things and the deepest things. As if it were a straight road mapped out on the ground, the first book is called the Ground Book.

Second is the Book of Water. With water as the basis, the spirit becomes like water. Water adopts the shape of its receptacle, it is sometimes a trickle and sometimes a wild

sea. Water has a clear blue colour. By the clarity, things of Ichi school are shown in this book. If you master the principles of sword-fencing, when you freely beat one man, you beat any man in the world. The spirit of defeating a man is the same for ten million men. The strategist makes small things into big things, like building a great Buddha from a one-foot model. I cannot write in detail how this is done. The principle of strategy is having one thing, to know ten thousand things. Things of the Ichi school are written in this, the Book of Water.

Third is the Book of Fire. This book is about fighting. The spirit of fire is fierce, whether the fire be small or big;

and so it is with battles. The Way of battles is the same for man to man fights and for ten-thousand-a-side battles. You must appreciate that spirit can become big or small. What is big is easy to perceive: what is small is difficult to perceive. In short, it is difficult for large numbers of men to change position, so their movements can be easily predicted. An individual can easily change his mind, so his movements are difficult to predict. You must appreciate this. The essence of this book is that you must train day and night in order to make quick decisions. In strategy, it is necessary to treat training as a part of normal life with

your spirit unchanging. Thus, combat in battle is described in the Book of Fire.

Fourthly the Book of Wind. This book is not concerned with my Ichi school, but with other schools of strategy. By Wind, I mean old traditions, present-day traditions, and family traditions of strategy. Thus I clearly explain the strategies of the world. This is tradition. It is difficult to know yourself if you do not know others. To all Ways there are side tracks. If you study a Way daily, and your spirit diverges, you may think you are obeying a good way, but objectively it is not the true Way. If you are following the true Way and diverge a little, this will later become a large divergence. You must realize this. Other strategies have come to be thought of as mere sword-fencing, and it is not unreasonable that this should be so. The benefit of my strategy, although it includes sword-fencing, lies in a separate principle. I have explained what is commonly meant by strategy in other schools in the Tradition [Wind] Book.

Fifthly, the Book of the Void. By Void, I mean that which has no beginning and no end. Attaining this principle means not attaining the principle. The Way of strategy is the Way of nature. When you appreciate the power of nature, knowing the rhythm of any situation, you will be able to hit the enemy naturally and strike naturally. All this is the Way of the Void. I intend to show how to follow the true Way according to nature in the Book of the Void.

Niten Ichi-ryū Ni To (one school – two swords)

Warriors, both commanders and troopers, carry two swords at their belt. In olden times these were called the long sword and the sword; nowadays they are known as the sword and the companion sword. Let it suffice to say that in our land, whatever the reason, a warrior carries two swords at his belt. It is the Way of the warrior. Niten Ichi-ryū shows the advantage of using both swords.

The spear and halberd are weapons which are carried out of doors. Students of the Ichi school Way of strategy should train from the start with the sword and long sword in either hand. This is the truth: when you sacrifice your life, you must make fullest use of your weaponry. It is false not to do so, and to die with a weapon yet undrawn.

If you hold a sword with both hands, it is difficult to wield it freely to left and right, so my method is to carry the sword in one hand. This does not apply to large weapons such as the spear or halberd, but swords and companion swords can be carried in one hand. It is encumbering to

hold a sword in both hands when you are on horseback, when running on uneven roads, on swampy ground, muddy rice fields, stony ground, or in a crowd of people. To hold the long sword in both hands is not the true Way, for if you carry a bow or spear or other arms in your left hand you have only one hand free for the long sword. However, when it is difficult to cut an enemy down with one hand, you must use both hands. It is not difficult to wield a sword in one hand; the Way to learn this is to train with two long swords, one in each hand. It will seem difficult at first, but everything is difficult at first. Bows are difficult to draw, halberds are difficult to wield; as you become accustomed to the bow so your pull will become stronger. When you become used to wielding the long sword, you will gain the power of the Way and wield the sword well.

As I will explain in the second book, the Book of Water, there is no fast way of wielding the long sword. The long sword should be wielded broadly, and the companion sword closely. This is the first thing to realize.

According to this Ichi school, you can win with a long weapon, and yet you can also win with a short weapon. In short, the Way of the Ichi school is the spirit of winning, whatever the weapon and whatever its size.

It is better to use two swords rather than one when you are fighting a crowd, and especially if you want to take a prisoner.

These things cannot be explained in detail. From one thing, know ten thousand things. When you attain the Way of strategy there will not be one thing you cannot see. You must study hard.

The Virtue of the Long Sword

Masters of the long sword are called strategists. As for the other military arts, those who master the bow are called archers, those who master the spear are called spearmen, those who master the gun are called marksmen, those who master the halberd are called halberdiers. But we do not call masters of the Way of the long sword 'long-swordsmen', nor do we speak of 'companion-swordsmen'. Because bows, guns, spears and halberds are all warriors' equipment, they are certainly part of strategy. To master the virtue of the long sword is to govern the world and oneself, thus the long sword is the basis of strategy. The principle is 'strategy by means of the long sword'. If he attains the virtue of the long sword, one man can beat ten men. Just as one man can beat ten, so a hundred men can beat a thousand, and a thousand

men can beat ten thousand. In my strategy, one man is the same as ten thousand, so this strategy is the complete warrior's craft.

The Way of the warrior does not include other Ways, such as Confucianism, Buddhism, certain traditions, artistic accomplishments and dancing. But even though these are not part of the Way, if you know the Way broadly you will see it in everything. Men must polish their particular Way.

The Benefit of Weapons in Strategy

There is a time and a place for use of weapons.

The best use of the companion sword is in a confined space, or when you are engaged closely with an opponent. The long sword can be used effectively in all situations.

The halberd is inferior to the spear on the battlefield. With the spear, you can take the initiative; the halberd is defensive. In the hands of one of two men of equal ability, the spear gives a little extra strength. Spear and halberd both have their uses, but neither is very beneficial in confined spaces. They cannot be used for taking a prisoner. They are essentially weapons for the field.

Anyway, if you learn 'indoor' techniques, you will think narrowly and forget the true Way. Thus, you will have difficulty in actual encounters.

The bow is tactically strong at the commencement of battle, especially battles on a moor, as it is possible to shoot quickly from among the spearmen. However, it is unsatisfactory in sieges, or when the enemy is more than forty yards away. For this reason there are now few traditional schools of archery. There is little use today for this kind of skill.

From inside fortifications, the gun has no equal among weapons. It is the supreme weapon on the field before the

ranks clash, but once swords are crossed the gun becomes useless. One of the virtues of the bow is that you can see the arrows in flight and correct your aim accordingly, whereas gunshot cannot be seen. You must appreciate the importance of this.

Just as a horse must have endurance and no defects, so it is with weapons. Horses should walk strongly, and swords and companion swords should cut strongly. Spears and halberds must stand up to heavy use: bows and guns must be sturdy. Weapons should be hardy rather than decorative.

You should not have a favourite weapon. To become over-familiar with one weapon is as much a fault as not knowing it sufficiently well. You should not copy others, but use weapons which you can handle properly. It is bad for commanders and troopers to have likes and dislikes. These are things you must learn thoroughly.

Timing in Strategy

There is timing in everything. Timing in strategy cannot be mastered without a great deal of practice.

Timing is important in dancing and pipe or string music, for they are in rhythm only if timing is good. Timing and rhythm are also involved in the military arts, shooting bows

and guns, and riding horses. In all skills and abilities there is timing. There is also timing in the Void.

There is timing in the whole life of the warrior, in his thriving and declining, in his harmony and discord. Similarly, there is timing in the Way of the merchant, in the rise and fall of capital. All things entail rising and falling timing. You must be able to discern this. In strategy, there are various timing considerations. From the outset, you must know the applicable timing and the inapplicable timing, and from among the large and small things and the fast and slow timings find the relevant timing, first seeing the distance timing and the background timing. This is

the main thing in strategy. It is especially important to know the background timing, otherwise your strategy will become uncertain.

You win in battles with the timing in the Void born of the timing of cunning by knowing the enemies' timing, and thus using a timing which the enemy does not expect.

All the five books are chiefly concerned with timing. You must train sufficiently to appreciate all this.

If you practise day and night in the above Ichi school strategy, your spirit will naturally broaden. In this manner, large-scale strategy and the strategy of hand-to-hand combat is propagated in the world. This is recorded for the first time in the five books of Ground, Water, Fire, Tradition (Wind) and Void. This is the Way for men who want to learn my strategy:

1. Do not think dishonestly.
2. The Way is in training.
3. Become acquainted with every art.
4. Know the Ways of all professions.
5. Distinguish between gain and loss in worldly matters.
6. Develop intuitive judgement and understanding for everything.

7. Perceive those things which cannot be seen.
8. Pay attention even to trifles.
9. Do nothing which is of no use.

It is important to start by setting these broad principles in your heart, and train in the Way of strategy. If you do not look at things on a large scale it will be difficult for you to master strategy. If you learn and attain this strategy you will never lose even to twenty or thirty enemies. More than anything to start with you must set your heart on strategy and earnestly stick to the Way. You will come to be able actually to beat men in fights, and win with your eye. Also by training you will be able to control your own body freely, conquer men with your body, and with sufficient training you will be able to beat ten men with your spirit. When you have reached this point, will it not mean that you are invincible?

Moreover, in large-scale strategy the superior man will manage many subordinates dexterously, bear himself correctly, govern the country and foster the people, thus preserving the ruler's discipline. If there is a Way involving the spirit of not being defeated, to help oneself and gain honour, it is the Way of strategy.

STRATEGY AND VISION

One of *The Book of Five Rings*' overarching themes is the need to formulate a well-defined vision and strategy for any endeavour undertaken, marked by discipline, dedication, patience and flexibility. This is outlined by Musashi in 'The Book of the Ground', the first of his *Five Rings*.

Musashi develops his idea that the Way of strategy transcends sword-fencing techniques – and for today's entrepreneur, the double-bladed swordsmanship he is synonymous with should be seen as the allegorical vehicle through which he has chosen to communicate his wider meaning. The 'Way of the warrior' he consistently refers to and asks that we aspire to is marked by the mastery of numerous disciplines, not the command of one. The lesson

to be learned from this is that to be successful one must wear many hats.

While he communicates the 'how', 'why' and 'when' of an action or event using examples of weaponry, the modern-day application of Musashi's words has come to transcend the use of swords, bows and halberds. Entrepreneurs should look beyond the passages as a straightforward manual on pugilism to view it instead as a guide to crafting and achieving the right vision by implementing the correct strategy. This right vision will acknowledge one's strengths and weaknesses and asks that one's internal dialogue is an honest one to hit on our best parts for maximum resonance and advantage. Just as Musashi describes: 'You should not copy others, but use weapons which you can handle properly.'

A key theme here is that no one-size-fits-all approach is to be taken. Rather, the student must adopt their own 'Way'. As Musashi makes clear: 'If you know the Way broadly you will see it in everything. Men must polish their particular Way.'

He tells us to, 'Know the smallest things and the biggest things, the shallowest things and the deepest things.'

The entrepreneurially minded can take from this that they must onboard as much as possible to create from that infinite mix a strategic concoction that works to channel their strengths, rather than aping something that has worked for someone else. Otherwise, it will be like trying to force a square peg into a round hole.

Musashi also fires a warning shot across the ages that confirmation bias must be avoided when he remarks that,

'You should not have a favourite weapon. To become over-familiar with one weapon is as much a fault as not knowing it sufficiently well.'

And in stating that 'It is bad for commanders and troopers to have likes and dislikes,' he says to today's entrepreneur that it is essential to select the correct tactics and personnel for the task at hand. And, if we ourselves do not have the requisite skill set to do so, then we must be humble enough to delegate to someone who has.

No Timewasters Please

For Musashi, substance over style is key. When he says that 'Weapons should be hardy rather than decorative,' he is reconfirming the importance of deploying the right tools for the job. It is the only way to gain a complete picture of the business landscape and create the strategic vision that all stakeholders can collect around.

More specifically, this means gaining an intimate under-standing of the market via comprehensive research to include analysis of the competition. This ensures clear opportunities can be identified, and a unique value proposition developed to exploit them to meet the target audience's needs and preferences, perhaps with a view to leveraging emerging trends or technologies in pursuit of early advantage. A roadmap can be created from this that aligns actions with goals.

For Musashi, nothing can be gained from showboating, spin or hyperbole, since one will soon get found out by one's

opponent. The same applies to even the slickest entrepreneur if the next big thing they are peddling is just hot air. The market will find them out. Those looking for a shortcut to success, or hoping to skip the hard work and endless practice necessary to hone their skills, are likely to be disappointed. Musashi the master strategist looks dimly upon those 'colouring and showing off their technique, trying to hasten the bloom of the flower'.

Musashi's strategic vision acts as a lodestar to assist with decision-making and prioritizing. Without a guiding light, it is nigh-on impossible to collectively inspire the workforce and keep things on course.

Courage and Connection

This idea that there is more than one way to operate in business informed by a unique strategy seems far from radical today, but in Musashi's seventeenth-century Japan, each aspect of life was so prescriptive and regulated, the notion that you could go your own way would have been considered highly unusual.

Even today, despite the prevailing belief we have the freedom to think and do as we please – at least in certain countries – those considered too far-out are still readily consigned to the socio-economic wilderness.

In other words, today's entrepreneur, just like the warrior class Musashi was speaking to in his day, must be prepared to tear down the walls and dispense with conventional wisdom sufficient to let the good stuff in – yet not so much that they

lose the ability to communicate, or to communicate effectively enough to be understood by others yet to make the journey.

Musashi identifies timing as being of crucial importance in 'The Book of the Ground'. Knowing when to strike and when to hold back is as important today for those looking to unleash their new product or service on to the market as it was for warriors seeking to win duels when *The Book of Five Rings* was written. As he says: 'Timing in strategy cannot be mastered without a great deal of practice.'

Musashi also attaches great importance to training and sees it as being central to cultivating the quality of discernment that allows warriors to select the correct response to get the better of their opponent. Knowing what to do in theory is one thing; doing it in practice is something else entirely. As Musashi notes, 'The Way is in training', which increases one's capacity to make the right move. Also, only through rigorous and relentless training can a person's natural authority and gravitas slowly form and develop to a point where others can begin to believe in, trust and follow them.

Everything Everywhere All at Once

For the twenty-first-century entrepreneur, Musashi's training equates to continuous learning and improvement, whereby new skills and knowledge are developed alongside the reinforcement of what has been learned to date to create within oneself an infectious culture of innovation. And when he says 'Become acquainted with every art,' those seeking to make headway in the modern business arena can take from

this that they should look beyond both their own role and their core business to gain an understanding of how other industries overcome challenges.

Richard Branson, the British business magnate and founder of the Virgin Group, has expressed his admiration for *The Book of Five Rings*, crediting Musashi's principles with shaping his own entrepreneurial mindset and strategic decision-making. His multi-faceted empire, which includes businesses as disparate as gymnasiums, airlines, financial services and telecommunications within its portfolio, is a prime example of the merits of the growth mindset Musashi espouses. As the Virgin Group founder had remarked: 'You don't learn to walk by following rules. You learn by doing and by falling over.'

To illustrate his position better, Musashi dedicates a whole section in 'The Book of the Ground' to comparing the Way of the carpenter to strategy. Records show that he had knowledge of architecture. So, this was a natural analogy for him. He speaks of the need to have a broad knowledge of everything to plan, construct and realize a building – of knowing who to delegate responsibility to; of allocating jobs to those most capable of carrying them out determined by their specific skill sets and temperament; of knowing which resources to deploy and where to direct them. This skill – and with it, the increased scope for success – can only be developed through constant practice, for as Musashi explains: 'When the carpenter grows to be skilled and understands measures, he can become a foreman.'

While the carpenter in Musashi's mind was a metaphor for the warrior, today read 'entrepreneur' for a helpful visualization of how to be the architect of commercial success.

'The foreman carpenter allots his men work according to their ability', Musashi explains, and the message here is that everyone on the team has a vital role to play, even those with little in the way of experience. Building the business and realizing the architect's vision is all about teamwork. A sole trader mentality will only get the entrepreneur so far, because, if one wants to grow, sooner or later one will be called upon to lead and inspire.

Just as back then, so too today any group of individuals will be made up of self-starters and those requiring more direction. Identifying which team members require motivation and management, and which have the ingredients to be the motivators and the managers, is an essential skill. For Musashi, 'the foreman should … know their morale and spirit, and encourage them when necessary'. His advocacy for a holistic approach to work that views all forces as being interconnected and only comprehensible by reference to the whole underpins his thinking. It is encapsulated in the following passage: 'The attainment of the carpenter is that his work is not warped, that the joints are not misaligned, and that the work is truly planed so that it meets well and is not merely finished in sections.'

Musashi talks exclusively of men. While he was decidedly disruptive for his time, seventeenth-century Japan was marked by very clear roles for men and women, and crossing

the divide was unthinkable. Today, however, things are very different, and Musashi's teachings can be applied equally to both sexes. The multiversal view he adopts in his magnum opus is that anything and everything is possible and true discipline means being open, alert and adaptable to any conceivable development. This belief that 'when you attain the Way of strategy there will not be one thing you cannot see' favours no one group and will resonate with any entrepreneurially minded individual, regardless of how they identify.

Changing it Up

'The Book of the Ground' is – as the name suggests – concerned with foundations, fundamentals, of being and remaining 'grounded', and Musashi's two swords approach to combat is how he communicates his common-sense thinking.

To cut a long story short, two swords were traditionally sported by the warrior, yet only one was used, and with two hands. The other was decorative, idle, a back-up at best.

For Musashi, it is the height of folly to actively hamstring yourself in this way, simply because tradition dictates it must be so. The message is an incredibly potent one. If there is no present-day rationale for doing something a certain way, then dispense with that course of action and replace it with something better that will help you deliver on your objectives – in his case, victory in a duel and the avoidance of death.

When what's at stake is existential, the risks are high, be it for the warrior or the entrepreneur. If the latter does not feel

able to call on that which could bestow advantage, they raise the prospect of the small flame of a great business idea being snuffed out before it has a chance to take hold. This could potentially lead to a lesser product or service succeeding because someone else knew how to play the game and was prepared to make use of all of the tools at their disposal. 'This is the truth: when you sacrifice your life, you must make fullest use of your weaponry,' Musashi writes. 'It is false not to do so, and to die with a weapon yet undrawn.'

The master strategist acknowledges that old habits die hard but lets us know that it is eminently possible to reprogramme ourselves and learn new skills. 'It will seem difficult at first, but everything is difficult at first,' he says when he describes the advantages of training with and mastering the use of two long swords, one in each hand.

These days, once young adults leave formal education many get out of the habit of learning new things, but the true entrepreneur sees life as a constant learning curve and embraces the chance to broaden their understanding. Richard Branson, who seems to embody Musashi's Way, describes life as 'almost like one long university education that I never had – every day I'm learning something new'.

Embrace Excellence

Musashi also asserts in 'The Book of the Ground' that all is not lost even in the event one finds oneself disadvantaged, since there is more than one path to victory. For him, the right mindset was more important than the right weapons,

and entrepreneurs should understand that even though resources may be stretched, trading conditions bleak, or backers seemingly nowhere to be found, occupying the correct headspace that allows one to prioritize correctly and focus on the essential will see one through to more auspicious times. This thinking is encapsulated in Musashi's declaration that 'the Way of the Ichi school is the spirit of winning, whatever the weapon and whatever its size'.

For Musashi, the long sword was the conduit to effect and implement one's strategy, and so it transcended and was distinct from any other weapon. To see it as mere equipment was to fundamentally miss his point that the sword was an extension of the person wielding it – affording the opportunity through his two-sword approach to fuse mind, body and sword as one in perfect harmony. Elon Musk neatly framed Musashi's thinking for the present day when he said that, 'We are already cyborgs. Your phone and computer are extensions of you.'

While the importance and incorruptibility Musashi attaches to the sword is hard to fathom in today's commercial realm, where there are numerous instruments through which to showcase one's integrated credentials and realize one's goals, what we can take from these passages is that being a practitioner of excellence will allow us to make optimum use of the technologies and practices out there so that they work better for us than others. This will catalyze delivery of our strategy, enhance our ability to pivot to new conditions, and give us an edge over the competition.

Musk, for example, famously dedicates himself to multiple globally disruptive projects in parallel. Despite being initially ridiculed time and again for the ambition of his respective projects, his innate curiosity, dedication to the task at hand, pursuit of excellence, faith in his own systems, and his focus on practicality in lieu of mores and traditions has seen him become today's ultimate entrepreneur, personifying Musashi's spirit of winning and the virtue of the long sword, such that he 'govern[s] the world and [him]self'. The master would approve of this modern-day warrior's craftsmanship.

And in understanding and applying Musashi's principles, Musk has been able to relentlessly defy the odds, as convention sees them. His take on the world is that, 'If he attains the virtue of the long sword, one man can beat ten men. Just as one man can beat ten, so a hundred men can beat a thousand, and a thousand men can beat ten thousand. In my strategy, one man is the same as ten thousand.'

Although those are Musashi's words, they could just as well have been written by Musk.

Entrepreneurs tend to be restless figures, not known for their patience. But being enslaved to impulsiveness or an ungovernable will is to see one's goals recede into the distance. It is essential to be able to keep one's impatience in check. There is nothing stopping one being persistent in the quest to turns one's vision into reality, while at the same time exercising restraint and self-control. Failure to do so will result in ill-timed actions and adverse consequences.

Mastering the Art of Timing

Musashi makes clear that timing is everything, dedicating a whole section of 'The Book of the Ground' to the concept. The inexperienced warrior or entrepreneur will let the blood rush to their head in response to an unexpected challenge and meet it with a knee-jerk reaction. The trick, however, is to accept that headwinds are inevitable, and to roll with and ride out the storm, safe in the knowledge that, thanks to the strong foundations already laid and being in possession of a guiding mothership strategy, the clouds will clear and the right moment to strike will present itself.

It could be the warrior that forgets their training, letting down their guard to lash out in response to an offensive manoeuvre, only to expose themselves to mortal danger. Or it could be the entrepreneur that rushes a product to market despite having not yet secured the requisite budget to promote it, because everyone is asking when the next big thing is going to happen and they feel obliged to deliver something.

What unites these actors is that they have given in to stress, emotion, or the spirit of the moment.

Musashi stipulates that, 'From the outset, you must know the applicable timing and the inapplicable timing.' This is where the importance of training comes in, whereby 'your spirit will naturally broaden'.

Whether it's delivering a punchline, introducing a radical new government policy, or bringing to market something with the potential to change the world, get the timing wrong and the joke is sure to fall flat, the electorate may reject you,

or that iPhone impact you hoped for might end up instead being more of a Newton moment.

That you may not be familiar with the second Apple product mentioned above is just the point. The Newton personal digital assistant was announced too far in advance of its launch, and even by 1993, when it eventually hit the shelves, the market was not sufficiently familiar with such a device to feel comfortable paying somewhere in the region of $1,000 for one.

In 1972, Democratic presidential candidate George McGovern was soundly beaten to the top job by the incumbent Republican, Richard Nixon, despite the latter being associated with what had become a deeply unpopular war in Vietnam. McGovern was hoping to be voted in on a platform of immediately ending the war and of guaranteed minimum incomes for the poor.

While these messages would no doubt have resonated in certain elections to follow, such seemingly left-wing rhetoric in an era of Cold War anti-Communist paranoia meant it was always going to be an impossible sell at the time – especially when pitched against the backdrop of a strong US economy overseen by his opponent. As McGovern later observed, 'When they say you're ahead of your time, it's just a polite way of saying you have a real bad sense of timing.'

Allowing delusions of grandeur, flights of fancy, or one's own cultivated rhetoric to supersede logic and real-world conditions as decision-making drivers is the hallmark of an ungrounded entrepreneur. Similarly, Musashi saw how such

behaviour would cause the warrior to shift focus away from the moment, leading to a dulling of the senses. This would be marked by an inability to ascertain when and where to strike, when threats are incoming, in what form and how to repel them. 'There is timing in the whole life of the warrior,' Musashi wrote. 'In his thriving and declining, in his harmony and discord.'

At the end of 'The Book of the Ground' (see pages 43–44), Musashi lists what he believes should be the warrior's foundational principles: a list of pithy truths that could work as mantras for *The Book of Five Rings*. For the entrepreneur, they act as invaluable short form reference points to return to time and again if one is struggling to find 'the Way' but are pushed for time.

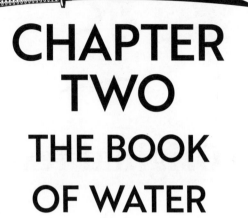

CHAPTER TWO

THE BOOK OF WATER

Original Text

The spirit of the Niten Ichi school of strategy is based on water, and this Book of Water explains methods of victory as the long-sword form of the Ichi school. Language does not extend to explaining the Way in detail, but it can be grasped intuitively. Study this book; read a word then ponder on it. If you interpret the meaning loosely, you will mistake the Way.

The principles of strategy are written down here in terms of single combat, but you must think broadly so that you attain an understanding for ten-thousand-a-side battles.

Strategy is different from other things in that if you mistake the Way even a little you will become bewildered and fall into bad ways.

If you merely read this book you will not reach the Way of strategy. Absorb the things written in this book. Do not just read, memorize or imitate, but study hard so that

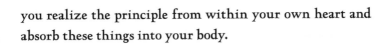

you realize the principle from within your own heart and absorb these things into your body.

Spiritual bearing in strategy

In strategy, your spiritual bearing must not be any different from normal. Both in fighting and in everyday life you should be determined though calm. Meet the situation without tenseness yet not recklessly, your spirit settled yet unbiased. Even when your spirit is calm do not let your body relax, and when your body is relaxed do not let your spirit slacken. Do not let your spirit be influenced by your body, or your body influenced by your spirit. Be neither

insufficiently spirited nor over-spirited. An elevated spirit is weak and a low spirit is weak. Do not let the enemy see your spirit.

Small people must be completely familiar with the spirit of large people, and large people must be familiar with the spirit of small people. Whatever your size, do not be misled by the reactions of your own body. With your spirit open and unconstricted, look at things from a high point of view. You must cultivate your wisdom and spirit. Polish your wisdom: learn public justice, distinguish between good and evil, study the Ways of different arts one by one. When you cannot be deceived by men you will have realized the wisdom of strategy.

The wisdom of strategy is different from other things. On the battlefield, even when you are hard-pressed, you should ceaselessly research the principles of strategy so that you can develop a steady spirit.

Stance in strategy

Adopt a stance with the head erect, neither hanging down, nor looking up, nor twisted. Your forehead and the space between your eyes should not be wrinkled. Do not roll your eyes nor allow them to blink, but slightly narrow them.

With your features composed, keep the line of your nose straight with a feeling of slightly flaring your nostrils. Hold the line of the rear of the neck straight: instil vigour into your hairline, and in the same way from the shoulders down through your entire body. Lower both shoulders and, without the buttocks jutting out, put strength into your legs from the knees to the tops of your toes. Brace your abdomen so that you do not bend at the hips. Wedge your companion sword in your belt against your abdomen, so that your belt is not slack – this is called 'wedging in'.

In all forms of strategy, it is necessary to maintain the combat stance in everyday life and to make your everyday stance your combat stance. You must research this well.

The gaze in strategy

The gaze should be large and broad. This is the twofold gaze, 'perception and sight'. Perception is strong and sight is weak.

In strategy, it is important to see distant things as if they were close and to take a distanced view of close things. It is important in strategy to know the enemy's sword and not to be distracted by insignificant movements of his sword. You must study this. The gaze is the same for single combat and for large-scale combat.

It is necessary in strategy to be able to look to both sides without moving the eyeballs. You cannot master this ability quickly. Learn what is written here; use this gaze in everyday life and do not vary it whatever happens.

Holding the long sword

Grip the long sword with a rather floating feeling in your thumb and forefinger, with the middle finger neither tight nor slack, and with the last two fingers tight. It is bad to have play in your hands.

When you take up a sword, you must feel intent on cutting the enemy. As you cut an enemy you must not change your grip, and your hands must not 'cower'. When

you dash the enemy's sword aside, or ward it off, or force it down, you must slightly change the feeling in your thumb and forefinger. Above all, you must be intent on cutting the enemy in the way you grip the sword.

The grip for combat and for sword-testing is the same. There is no such thing as a 'man-cutting grip'.

Generally, I dislike fixedness in both long swords and hands. Fixedness means a dead hand. Pliability is a living hand. You must bear this in mind.

Footwork

With the tips of your toes somewhat floating, tread firmly with your heels. Whether you move fast or slow, with large or small steps, your feet must always move as in normal walking. I dislike the three walking methods known as 'jumping-foot', 'floating-foot' and 'fixed-steps'.

So-called 'Yin-Yang foot' is important to the Way. Yin-Yang foot means not moving on only one foot. It means moving your feet left-right and right-left when cutting, withdrawing, or warding off a cut. You should not move on one foot preferentially.

The Five Attitudes

The Five Attitudes are: Upper, Middle, Lower, Right Side and Left Side. These are the five. Although attitude has these five dimensions, the one purpose of all of them is to cut the enemy. There are none but these five attitudes.

Whatever attitude you are in, do not be conscious of making the attitude; think only of cutting. Your attitude should be large or small according to the situation. Upper, Lower and Middle attitudes are decisive. Left Side and Right Side attitudes are fluid. Left and Right attitudes should be used if there is an obstruction overhead or to

one side. The decision to use Left or Right depends on the place.

The essence of the Way is this. To understand attitude, you must thoroughly understand the Middle attitude. The Middle attitude is the heart of the attitudes. If we look at strategy on a broad scale, the Middle attitude is the seat of the commander, with the other four attitudes following the commander. You must appreciate this.

The Way of the long sword

Knowing the Way of the long sword means we can wield with two fingers the sword we usually carry. If we know the path of the sword well, we can wield it easily. If you try to wield the long sword quickly, you will mistake the Way. To wield the long sword well you must wield it calmly. If you try to wield it quickly, like a folding fan or a short sword, you will err by using 'short sword chopping'. You cannot cut a man with a long sword using this method.

When you have cut downwards with the long sword, lift it straight upwards; when you cut sideways, return the sword along a sideways path. Return the sword in a reasonable way, always stretching the elbows broadly. Wield the sword strongly.

This is the Way of the long sword.

If you learn to use the five approaches of my strategy, you will be able to wield a sword well. You must train constantly.

The Five Approaches

1. The first approach is the Middle attitude. Confront the enemy with the point of your sword against his face. When he attacks, dash his sword to the right and 'ride' it. Or, when the enemy attacks, deflect the point of his sword by hitting downwards, keeping your long sword where it is, and as the enemy renews the attack cut his arms from below. This is the first method.

   The five approaches are this kind of thing. You must train repeatedly using a long sword in order to learn them. When you master my Way of the long sword, you will be able to control any attack the enemy makes. I assure you, there are no attitudes other than the five attitudes of the long sword of Ni To.

2. In the second approach with the long sword, from the Upper attitude cut the enemy just as he attacks. If the enemy evades the cut, keep your sword where it is and, scooping from below, cut him as he renews the attack. It is possible to repeat the cut from here.

In this method, there are various changes in timing and spirit. You will be able to understand this by training in the Ichi school. You will always win with the five long sword methods. You must train repeatedly.

3. In the third approach, adopt the Lower attitude, anticipating scooping up. When the enemy attacks, hit his hands from below. As you do so, he may try to hit your sword down. If this is the case, cut his upper arm(s) horizontally with a feeling of 'crossing'. This means that from the Lower attitudes you hit the enemy at the instant that he attacks.

   You will encounter this method often, both as a beginner and in later strategy. You must train holding a long sword.

4. In this fourth approach, adopt the Left Side attitude. As the enemy attacks, hit his hands from below. If, as you hit his hands, he attempts to dash down your sword, with the feeling of hitting his hands, parry the path of his long sword and cut across from above your shoulder.

   This is the Way of the long sword. Through this method, you win by parrying the line of the enemy's attack. You must study this.

5. In the fifth approach, the sword is in the Right Side attitude. In accordance with the enemy's attack, cross your sword from below at the side to the Upper attitude. Then cut straight from above. This method is essential for knowing the Way of the long sword well. If you can use this method, you can freely wield a heavy long sword.

I cannot describe in detail how to use these five approaches. You must become well acquainted with my 'in harmony with the long sword' Way, learn large-scale timing, understand the enemy's long sword, and become used to the five approaches from the outset. You will always win by using these five methods, with various timing considerations discerning the enemy's spirit. You must consider all this carefully.

The Attitude-No-Attitude teaching

Attitude-No-Attitude means that there is no need for what are known as long sword attitudes.

Even so, attitudes exist as the five ways of holding the long sword. However you hold the sword, it must be in such a way that it is easy to cut the enemy well, in accordance with the situation, the place, and your relation to the enemy. From

the Upper attitude, as your spirit lessens you can adopt the Middle attitude, and from the Middle attitude you can raise the sword a little in your technique and adopt the Upper attitude. From the Lower attitude, you can raise the sword a little and adopt the Middle attitudes as the occasion demands. According to the situation, if you turn your sword from either the Left Side or Right Side attitude towards the centre, the Middle or the Lower attitude results.

The principle of this is called 'Existing Attitude – Non-existing Attitude'.

The primary thing when you take a sword in your hands is your intention to cut the enemy, whatever the means.

Whenever you parry, hit, spring, strike or touch the enemy's cutting sword, you must cut the enemy in the same movement. It is essential to attain this. If you think only of hitting, springing, striking or touching the enemy, you will not be able actually to cut him. More than anything, you must be thinking of carrying your movement through to cutting him. You must thoroughly research this.

Attitude in strategy on a larger scale is called 'battle array'. Such attitudes are all for winning battles. Fixed formation is bad. Study this well.

To hit the enemy 'in one timing'

'In one timing' means, when you have closed with the enemy, to hit him as quickly and directly as possible, without moving your body or settling your spirit, while you see that he is still undecided. The timing of hitting before the enemy decides to withdraw, break or hit, is this 'in one timing'.

You must train to achieve this timing, to be able to hit in the timing of an instant.

The 'abdomen timing of two'

When you attack and the enemy quickly retreats, as you see him tense you must feint a cut. Then, as he relaxes, follow up and hit him. This is the 'abdomen timing of two'.

It is very difficult to attain this merely by reading this book, but you will soon understand with a little instruction.

'No design, no conception'

In this method, when the enemy attacks and you also decide to attack, hit with your body, and hit with your spirit, and hit from the Void with your hands, accelerating strongly. This is the 'no design, no conception' cut.

This is the most important method of hitting. It is often used. You must train hard to understand it.

The 'flowing water' cut

The 'flowing water' cut is used when you are struggling blade to blade with the enemy. When he breaks and quickly withdraws, trying to spring with his long sword, expand your body and spirit and cut him as slowly as possible with your long sword, following your body like stagnant water. You can cut with certainty if you learn this. You must discern the enemy's grade.

The 'continuous' cut

When you attack and the enemy also attacks and your swords spring together, in one action cut his head, hands and legs. When you cut several places with one sweep of the long sword, it is the 'continuous' cut. You must practise this cut; it is often used. With detailed practice you should be able to understand it.

The 'fire and stones' cut

The 'fire and stones' cut means that when the enemy's long sword and your long sword clash together, you cut as

strongly as possible without raising the sword even a little. This means cutting quickly with the hands, body and legs – all three cutting strongly. If you train well enough you will be able to strike strongly.

The 'red leaves' cut

The 'red leaves' cut (alluding to falling, dying leaves) means knocking down the enemy's long sword. The spirit should be getting control of his sword. When the enemy is in a long-sword attitude in front of you and intent on cutting, hitting and parrying, you strongly hit the enemy's sword with the 'fire and stones' cut, perhaps in the design of the 'no design, no conception' cut. If you then beat down the point of his sword with a sticky feeling, he will necessarily drop the sword. If you practise this cut, it becomes easy to make the enemy drop his sword. You must train repetitively.

The 'body in place of the long sword'

Also the 'long sword in place of the body'. Usually we move the body and the sword at the same time to cut the enemy. However, according to the enemy's cutting method, you can dash against him with your body first, and afterwards cut with the sword. If his body is immovable, you can cut first

with the long sword, but generally you hit first with the body and then cut with the long sword. You must research this well and practise hitting.

'Cut and slash'

To 'cut and slash' are two different things. Cutting, whatever form of cutting it is, is decisive, with a resolute spirit. Slashing is nothing more than touching the enemy. Even if you slash strongly, and even if the enemy dies instantly, it is slashing. When you cut, your spirit is resolved. You must appreciate this. If you first slash the enemy's hands or legs, you must then cut strongly. Slashing is in spirit the same as touching. When you realize this, they become indistinguishable. Learn this well.

'Chinese monkey's body'

The 'Chinese monkey's body' is the spirit of not stretching out your arms. The spirit is to get in quickly, without in the least extending your arms, before the enemy cuts. If you are intent upon not stretching out your arms, you are effectively far away; the spirit is to go in with your whole body. When you come to within arm's reach it becomes easy to move your body in. You must research this well.

'Glue and lacquer emulsion body'

The spirit of 'glue and lacquer emulsion body' is to stick to the enemy and not separate from him. When you approach the enemy, stick firmly with your head, body and legs. People tend to advance their head and legs quickly, but their body lags behind. You should stick firmly so that there is not the slightest gap between the enemy's body and your body. You must consider this carefully.

'To strive for height'

By 'to strive for height' is meant, when you close with the enemy, to strive with him for superior height without

cringing. Stretch your legs, stretch your hips, and stretch your neck face to face with him. When you think you have won, and you are the higher, thrust in strongly. You must learn this.

'To apply stickiness'

When the enemy attacks and you also attack with the long sword, you should go in with a sticky feeling and fix your long sword against the enemy's as you receive his cut. The spirit of stickiness is not hitting very strongly, but hitting so that the long swords do not separate easily. It is best to approach as calmly as possible when hitting the enemy's long sword with stickiness. The difference between 'stickiness' and 'entanglement' is that stickiness is firm and entanglement is weak. You must appreciate this.

The 'body strike'

The 'body strike' means to approach the enemy through a gap in his guard. The spirit is to strike him with your body. Turn your face a little aside and strike the enemy's breast with your left shoulder thrust out. Approach with a spirit of bouncing the enemy away, striking as strongly as possible in time with your breathing. If you achieve this method of

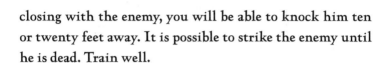

closing with the enemy, you will be able to knock him ten or twenty feet away. It is possible to strike the enemy until he is dead. Train well.

Three ways to parry his attack

There are three methods to parry a cut:

First, by dashing the enemy's long sword to your right, as if thrusting at his eyes, when he makes an attack;

Or to parry by thrusting the enemy's long sword towards his right eye with the feeling of snipping his neck;

Or, when you have a short 'long sword', without worrying about parrying the enemy's long sword, to close with him quickly, thrusting at his face with your left hand.

These are the three ways of parrying. You must bear in mind that you can always clench your left hand and thrust at the enemy's face with your fist. It is necessary to train well.

'To stab at the face'

'To stab at the face' means, when you are in confrontation with the enemy, that your spirit is intent on stabbing at his face, following the line of the blades with the point of your long sword. If you are intent on stabbing at his face, his face and body will become rideable. When the enemy becomes rideable, there are various opportunities for winning. You must concentrate on this. When fighting and the enemy's body becomes as if rideable, you can win quickly, so you ought not to forget to stab at the face. You must pursue the value of this technique through training.

'To stab at the heart'

'To stab at the heart' means, when fighting and there are obstructions above or to the sides, and whenever it is difficult to cut, to thrust at the enemy. You must stab the enemy's breast without letting the point of your long sword waver, showing the enemy the ridge of the blade square-on, and with the spirit of deflecting his long sword. The spirit of this principle is often useful when we become tired or for some reason our long sword will not cut. You must understand the application of this method.

'To scold "Tut-TUT!"'

'Scold' means that, when the enemy tries to counter-cut
as you attack, you counter-cut again from below as if
thrusting at him, trying to hold him down. With very
quick timing you cut, scolding the enemy. Thrust up,
'Tut!', and cut 'TUT!' This timing is encountered time and
time again in exchanges of blows. The way to scold Tut-
TUT is to time the cut simultaneously with raising your
long sword as if to thrust the enemy. You must learn this
through repetitive practice.

The 'smacking parry'

By 'smacking parry' is meant that when you clash swords
with the enemy, you meet his attacking cut on your long
sword with a tee-dum, tee-dum rhythm, smacking his sword
and cutting him. The spirit of the smacking parry is not
parrying, or smacking strongly, but smacking the enemy's
long sword in accordance with his attacking cut, primarily
intent on quickly cutting him. If you understand the
timing of smacking, however hard your long swords clash
together, your sword point will not be knocked back even a
little. You must research sufficiently to realize this.

'There are many enemies'

'There are many enemies' applies when you are fighting one against many. Draw both sword and companion sword and assume a wide-stretched left and right attitude. The spirit is to chase the enemies around from side to side, even though they come from all four directions. Observe their attacking order, and go to meet first those who attack first. Sweep your eyes around broadly, carefully examining the attacking order, and cut left and right alternately with your swords. Waiting is bad. Always quickly reassume your attitudes to both sides, cut the enemies down as they advance, crushing them in the direction from which they attack. Whatever you do, you must drive the enemy together, as if tying a line of fishes, and when they are seen to be piled up, cut them down strongly without giving them room to move.

The advantage when coming to blows

You can know how to win through strategy with the long sword, but it cannot be clearly explained in writing. You must practise diligently in order to understand how to win.

Oral tradition: 'The true Way of strategy is revealed in the long sword.'

'One cut'

You can win with certainty with the spirit of 'one cut'. It is difficult to attain this if you do not learn strategy well. If you train well in this Way, strategy will come from your heart and you will be able to win at will. You must train diligently.

'Direct communication'

The spirit of 'direct communication' is how the true Way of the Nito Ichi school is received and handed down.

Oral tradition: 'Teach your body strategy.'

To learn how to win with the long sword in strategy, first learn the five approaches and the five attitudes, and absorb the Way of the long sword naturally in your body. You must understand spirit and timing, handle the long sword naturally, and move body and legs in harmony with your spirit. Whether beating one man or two, you will then know values in strategy.

Study the contents of this book, taking one item at a time, and through fighting with enemies you will gradually come to know the principle of the Way.

Deliberately, with a patient spirit, absorb the virtue of all this, from time to time raising your hand in combat.

Maintain this spirit whenever you cross swords with an enemy.

Step by step walk the thousand-mile road.

Study strategy over the years and achieve the spirit of the warrior. Today is victory over yourself of yesterday; tomorrow is your victory over lesser men. Next, in order to beat more skilful men, train according to this book, not allowing your heart to be swayed along a side track. Even if you kill an enemy, if it is not based on what you have learned it is not the true Way.

If you attain this Way of victory, then you will be able to beat several tens of men. What remains is sword-fighting ability, which you can attain in battles and duels.

GO WITH
THE FLOW

At first glance, Musashi's second book, 'The Book of Water', seems to be concerned more or less exclusively with sword technique.

There's much talk of how to cut, slash, strike, hit, stab and parry. Yet, from behind this veneer of process, procedure and form can be gleaned a deeper meaning where water stands for fluidity and the need for the warrior to be able to readily shift position both mentally and physically to find the path of least resistance. The modern-day entrepreneur too must be able to fluidly adapt to any set of forces they are confronted with. As self-made rags-to-riches country music icon and Dollywood theme park owner Dolly Parton said, 'We cannot direct the wind, but we can adjust the sails.'

In occupying Musashi's state of being present and aware, the businessperson can readily apply and scale their instructions for one-to-one combat to much larger battles in the marketplace. As he says, 'The principles of strategy are written down here in terms of single combat, but you must think broadly so that you attain an understanding for ten-thousand-a-side battles.'

And the pearls of wisdom he kicks off 'The Book of Water' with don't stop there. In language that would not be out of place in a contemporary self-help bestseller, Musashi urges us to do more than simply go through the motions after reading his words. The capacity to effect positive change is only accessible to those prepared to assimilate it and change the way they operate in response. This is apparent to us when he says, 'Do not just read, memorize or imitate, but study hard so that you realize the principle from within your own heart and absorb these things into your body.'

American novelist and essayist Donna Tartt ventures something similar in her most famous work, *The Secret History*, when she says that, 'It is better to know one book intimately than a hundred superficially.'

Musashi dedicates much space to the idea of all things being in equilibrium through his idea of spiritual balance. He promotes concepts such as tranquillity and calmness, as one would expect from someone schooled in Buddhist thinking.

The State of Serenity

His focus on cultivating the correct temperament and being in perfect spiritual harmony is just as applicable for the warrior he was writing for as it is for enterprising types today. Top US life and business strategist Tony Robbins echoes Musashi's sentiment when he says that, 'Business is a spiritual pursuit. Your business will not grow unless you grow as a person.'

Achieving spiritual balance leads not only to the ability to be ready for and able to interpret anything that comes one's way and from any direction, but also allows for shielding one's intentions and weaknesses from opponents and competitors. It demands you have no preconceived notions that may cause you to favour one position or another, whereby 'your spirit [is] ... open and unconstricted ... settled yet unbiased'.

One's heightened ability to identify dishonesty will be the mark of progress in respect of enhanced spiritual bearing. For, as Musashi notes, 'When you cannot be deceived by men you will have realized the wisdom of strategy.'

Equally, knowledge of spirit means it will be possible to take advantage of those in a state of disequilibrium whose weaknesses have been exposed. In economics, the concept of market disequilibrium refers to a state where price movements cause an imbalance between supply and demand; so, like the warrior, the entrepreneur can introduce or exploit new opportunities for gain.

Entwined within the lessons on technique in 'The Book of Water' can be found life lessons that collectively hold in

the highest esteem the ability to hear, see or think accurately and clearly. Developing such acuity requires one to be always on high alert to one's surroundings. As Musashi puts it: 'In all forms of strategy, it is necessary to maintain the combat stance in everyday life and to make your everyday stance your combat stance.'

Musashi seems to have invested little time in achieving what we would now describe as a healthy work/life balance and is unlikely to have ceded there was ever an appropriate occasion to lower one's guard. Not for him any rest and relaxation.

Today, few save the most work-obsessed would suggest downtime was a weakness. The majority of people would surely agree with talk show legend Oprah Winfrey's assertion that she had, 'learned that you can't have everything and do everything at the same time'. However, what we can take from Musashi is that helpful techniques learned in the workplace can inform one's life outside of work, and vice-versa. This will allow us to become temperamentally consistent, rather than having a split work/life personality, which is dysfunctional and will act to retard progress towards one's goals.

From Looking to Seeing

Musashi attaches a great deal of importance to adopting the correct gaze. What the eyes behold is not enough for him; just as crucial to his idea of vision is what the head and the heart perceive. It is what he calls 'the twofold gaze, perception and sight'.

He impresses upon the reader how important it is to step back to gain an overview of a situation. When he says, 'In strategy, it is important to see distant things as if they were close and to take a distanced view of close things,' Musashi shines a torch on the path that will allow one to see the wood for the trees and so be able to detect threats or opportunities from afar. In business, this may mean a new disruptive technology on the horizon, or perhaps changes in preference or taste informed by cultural shifts.

The big picture view also means the entrepreneur is better able to determine which immediate challenges to prioritize dealing with, and which instead are trifling concerns safely left alone, whereby we are not 'distracted by insignificant movements of [the enemy's] sword'.

The ability to be constantly alert to the forces at work around us comes, counter-intuitively, to those who know stillness rather than those who actively endeavour to know it all. A true state of calm is slow to develop and requires much practice. Those who master the technique will be able to sniff out opportunities and capitalize on them where others detect nothing and feel no compulsion to act. As Musashi says: 'It is necessary in strategy to be able to look to both sides without moving the eyeballs. You cannot master this ability quickly.'

A Flexible not Fixed Identity

In his guidance on how to hold the long sword, the overriding message we can take today from Musashi is that one must

not be fixed in thought or strategy. He disliked 'fixedness in both long swords and hands', promoting instead the use of a grip marked by 'a rather floating feeling'. A lack of flexibility for Musashi speaks to stubbornness, belligerence, a lack of imagination, fear, slow wittedness, and a closed mind – in other words, the worst possible conditions to be adaptable and responsive, or to mix things up.

Those that like what they know and know what they like made for poor samurai warriors when *The Book of Five Rings* was written. Almost 400 years later, such individuals make for terrible business warriors today.

Musashi also makes clear that committing to and carrying through on a course of action once one has settled on what to do is essential to deliver victory. Anything else is a weakness, and such uncertainty will be picked up on by one's own team, causing them to doubt the strategy they have been asked to help implement. It will also be noticed by the competition, which, like a predator, could determine that one is vulnerable and ready for the taking. Such indecisiveness could see one squeezed out of the market from a rival's invigorated and aggressive marketing and sales push, or perhaps neutralized via a hostile takeover.

So, listen to Musashi – especially his reminder that, 'When you take up a sword, you must feel intent on cutting the enemy.'

This extends to the entrepreneur's team, which must fully stand behind the final executive decision regardless of their previous personal views. It is encapsulated in the management

principle of 'disagree and commit'. Governments the world over rely on the principle to be able to pass laws and action their manifesto commitments.

Regarding intent, Musashi knew that mistakes could be fatal for the warrior and that calculated risk taking was not an option. For the entrepreneur, however, it is slightly different, since few decisions are of existential importance and many are reversible. As Amazon founder Jeff Bezos says: 'Most decisions should probably be made with somewhere around 70 per cent of the information you wish you had. If you wait for 90 per cent, in most cases, you're probably being slow.'

The Goal is Victory

To make their ideas happen and thereafter grow that which they've successfully realized, entrepreneurs must endeavour to keep it simple. One does not have to reinvent the wheel to become a successful entrepreneur. The focus instead should be on solving a sufficiently large market need.

Similarly, Musashi asks of the warrior that they don't make things too complicated. He reduces the areas to attack on the human body to five, which he calls 'attitudes'. The goal is victory, and the focus should be on incapacitating one's opponent as the best way to deliver on that objective. As he says, the purpose is to 'cut the enemy [and] there are none but these five attitudes'.

For the entrepreneur, they will gain advantage over the competition if they strike at the optimum point, which will be determined by the prevailing conditions at the moment

of attack. They must be mindful of the fact that what worked last time may be the wrong approach this time around. As Musashi says, it is 'according to the situation [and] depends on the place'.

While seemingly prescriptive, the knowledge Musashi seeks to impart is of no value unless one strikes at the right time, is alert to what may be incoming, and understands the tools one is wielding – in his case the long sword; for the entrepreneur, it is any number of processes designed to secure market advantage and eclipse the competition.

Blindly stabbing in hope of hitting the right spot is a stab in the dark. It is why he says that 'You must become well acquainted with my "in harmony with the long sword" Way, learn large-scale timing [and] understand the enemy's long sword.'

Musashi also reminds the reader to see the job through and not hold back when he says: 'More than anything, you must be thinking of carrying your movement through to cutting him.'

Reticence means one's incomplete actions have only succeeded in alerting the opponent to one's true intentions, so providing them with a chance to regroup. You may not get a second chance.

For both the warrior and entrepreneur, it is illogical to have an objective only to duck out just when victory is within one's grasp. The strong survive and the weak must be consumed. It is the natural law of the jungle, of the battleground, and of the marketplace.

While governments may choose to subsidize certain industries to protect the electorate's jobs as part of their socio-economic welfare remit (Germany is famous for doing just this), successful entrepreneurs are less likely to adopt such a noble and indulgent mindset, as it will most likely take them away from their objective to grow and prosper. There are plenty of ways to be honourable in business, just as there were for Musashi's samurai when duelling, but attempting to subvert the natural order of things is not one of them.

The same indecision one must avoid is also something to look out for in one's opponent. If they appear to be unsure, it means they lack focus and that represents a perfect time to strike. As Musashi notes: 'Hit him as quickly and directly as possible, without moving your body or settling your spirit, while you see that he is still undecided.'

Roman statesman and lawyer Cicero knew the dangers of not being decisive when he observed that, 'Indecision is the thief of opportunity.'

A half-hearted approach to growing one's business may lead to accidental advantage, but also to the drawing of wrong conclusions, and a mistaken belief carried forward as to the efficacy of that course of action. Musashi illustrates the point by distinguishing between cutting and slashing. 'Cutting, whatever form of cutting it is, is decisive, with a resolute spirit. Slashing is nothing more than touching the enemy. Even if you slash strongly, and even if the enemy dies instantly, it is slashing,' he remarks.

Realistic Dreamers

One of the most insightful passages in 'The Book of Water' is when Musashi is describing the 'flowing water' cut technique, where he tells us that we 'must discern the enemy's grade'. He recognizes how important it is to gauge what you're up against and indicates that there is nothing glorious in bravery that leads to defeat, because one wrongly assessed a foe's credentials at the outset. Similarly, in the marketplace it is essential to choose one's battles carefully. For example, hoping or expecting to oust an established market leader with enormous resources at their disposal is a foolhardy venture, and it is essential to ensure one's commercial objectives are realistic and achievable. As writer and activist Jonathan Kozol notes: 'Pick battles big enough to matter, small enough to win.'

For all his instructions on how best to go on the offensive, Musashi also reminds the reader that the opponent will have their own offensive agenda, and so dedicates space to describing the different ways to parry.

For entrepreneurs, it is just as important to be able to respond to assaults from without as it is to focus on realizing one's own ambitions. There are times for all businesses when they need to defend their interests – perhaps from a hostile takeover or to restore a tarnished reputation. Protecting what one has built up is just as important as growing it; the greater the range of potential responses to draw from, the more likely one will be able to repel all-comers. It is why the savvy investor never puts all their eggs in one basket when seeking

to preserve and grow their wealth, but instead favours a diversified portfolio weighted in accordance with their risk appetite and the prevailing economic winds of the day.

Musashi concludes 'The Book of Water' by reminding us that life is a journey in which one should never stop learning. Inertia achieves nothing, and one must keep moving forward. Or, as Musashi puts it: 'Step by step walk the thousand-mile road.'

In doing so, the entrepreneur will make great strides in their personal development, advances they can then bring to bear in their work, affording scope to compete with bigger players in the marketplace.

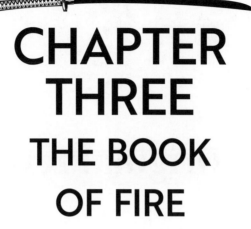

CHAPTER
THREE
THE BOOK
OF FIRE

Original Text

In this, the Book of Fire of the Nito Ichi
school of strategy, I describe fighting as fire.

In the first place, people think narrowly about the benefit of strategy. By using only their fingertips, they only know the benefit of three of the five inches of the wrist. They let a contest be decided, as with the folding fan, merely by the span of their forearms. They specialize in the small matter of dexterity, learning such trifles as hand and leg movements with the bamboo practice sword.

In my strategy, the training for killing enemies is by way of many contests, fighting for survival, discovering the meaning of life and death, learning the Way of the sword, judging the strength of attacks and understanding the Way of the 'edge and ridge' of the sword.

You cannot profit from small techniques, particularly when full armour is worn. My Way of strategy is the sure method to win when fighting for your life one man against

five or ten. There is nothing wrong with the principle 'one man can beat ten, so a thousand men can beat ten thousand'. You must research this. Of course, you cannot assemble a thousand or ten thousand men for everyday training. But you can become a master of strategy by training alone with a sword, so that you can understand the enemy's strategies, his strength and resources, and come to appreciate how to apply strategy to beat ten thousand enemies.

Any man who wants to master the essence of my strategy must research diligently, training morning and evening. Thus can he polish his skill, become free from self, and realize extraordinary ability. He will come to possess miraculous power.

This is the practical result of strategy.

Depending on the place

Examine your environment.

Stand in the sun; that is, take up an attitude with the sun behind you. If the situation does not allow this, you must try to keep the sun on your right side. In buildings, you must stand with the entrance behind you or to your right. Make sure that your rear is unobstructed, and that there is free space on your left, your right side being occupied with your sword attitude. At night, if the enemy can be seen, keep the fire behind you and the entrance to your right, and otherwise take up your attitude as above. You must look down on the enemy, and take up your attitude on slightly higher places. For example, the Kamiza in a house is thought of as a high place.

When the fight comes, always endeavour to chase the enemy around to your left side. Chase him towards awkward places, and try to keep him with his back to awkward places. When the enemy gets into an inconvenient position, do not let him look around, but conscientiously chase him around and pin him down. In houses, chase the enemy into the thresholds, lintels, doors, verandas, pillars, and so on, again not letting him see his situation.

Always chase the enemy into bad footholds, obstacles at

the side, and so on, using the virtues of the place to establish predominant positions from which to fight. You must research and train diligently in this.

The three methods to forestall the enemy

The first is to forestall him by attacking. This is called Ken No Sen [to set him up].

Another method is to forestall him as he attacks. This is called Tai No Sen [to wait for the initiative].

The other method is when you and the enemy attack together. This is called Tai Tai No Sen [to accompany him and forestall him].

There are no methods of taking the lead other than these three. Because you can win quickly by taking the lead, it is one of the most important things in strategy. There are several things involved in taking the lead. You must make the best of the situation, see through the enemy's spirit so that you grasp his strategy and defeat him. It is impossible to write about this in detail.

The first – Ken No Sen

When you decide to attack, keep calm and dash in quickly, forestalling the enemy. Or you can advance seemingly

strongly but with a reserved spirit, forestalling him with the reserve.

Alternatively, advance with as strong a spirit as possible, and when you reach the enemy move with your feet a little quicker than normal, unsettling him and overwhelming him sharply.

Or, with your spirit calm, attack with a feeling of constantly crushing the enemy, from first to last. The spirit is to win in the depths of the enemy.

These are all Ken No Sen.

The second – Tai No Sen

When the enemy attacks, remain undisturbed but feign weakness. As the enemy reaches you, suddenly move away indicating that you intend to jump aside, then dash in attacking strongly as soon as you see the enemy relax. This is one way.

Or, as the enemy attacks, attack more strongly, taking advantage of the resulting disorder in his timing to win.

This is the Tai No Sen principle.

The third – Tai Tai No Sen

When the enemy makes a quick attack, you must attack strongly and calmly, aim for his weak point as he draws near, and strongly defeat him.

Or, if the enemy attacks calmly, you must observe his movement and, with your body rather floating, join in with his movements as he draws near. Move quickly and cut him strongly.

This is Tai Tai No Sen.

These things cannot be clearly explained in words. You must research what is written here. In these three ways of forestalling, you must judge the situation. This does not mean that you always attack first; but if the enemy

attacks first you can lead him around. In strategy, you have effectively won when you forestall the enemy, so you must train well to attain this.

'To hold down a pillow'

'To hold down a pillow' means not allowing the enemy's head to rise.

In contests of strategy, it is bad to be led about by the enemy. You must always be able to lead the enemy about. Obviously, the enemy will also be thinking of doing this, but he cannot forestall you if you do not allow him to come out. In strategy, you must stop the enemy as he attempts to cut; you must push down his thrust, and throw off his hold when he tries to grapple. This is the meaning of 'to hold down a pillow'. When you have grasped this principle, whatever the enemy tries to bring about in the fight you will see in advance and suppress it. The spirit is to check his attack at the syllable 'at ...'; when he jumps, check his advance at the syllable 'ju ...'; and check his cut at 'cu ...'.

The important thing in strategy is to suppress the enemy's useful actions but allow his useless actions. However, doing this alone is defensive. First, you must act according to the Way, suppress the enemy's techniques, foil his plans, and

thence command him directly. When you can do this, you will be a master of strategy. You must train well and research 'holding down a pillow'.

'Crossing at a ford'

'Crossing at a ford' means, for example, crossing the sea at a strait, or crossing over a hundred miles of broad sea at a crossing place. I believe this 'crossing at a ford' occurs often in a man's lifetime. It means setting sail even though your friends stay in harbour, knowing the route, knowing the soundness of your ship and the favour of the day. When all the conditions are met, and there is perhaps a favourable wind, or a tailwind, then set sail. If the wind changes within a few miles of your destination, you must row across the remaining distance without sail.

If you attain this spirit, it applies to everyday life. You must always think of crossing at a ford.

In strategy, also, it is important to 'cross at a ford'. Discern the enemy's capability and, knowing your own strong points, 'cross the ford' at the advantageous place, as a good captain crosses a sea route. If you succeed in crossing at the best place, you may take your ease. To cross at a ford means to attack the enemy's weak point, and to put yourself in an

advantageous position. This is how to win in large-scale strategy. The spirit of crossing at a ford is necessary in both large- and small-scale strategy.

You must research this well.

'To know the times'

'To know the times' means to know the enemy's disposition in battle. Is it flourishing or waning? By observing the spirit of the enemy's men and getting the best position, you can work out the enemy's disposition and move your men accordingly. You can win through this principle of strategy, fighting from a position of advantage.

When in a duel, you must forestall the enemy and attack when you have first recognized his school of strategy, perceived his quality and his strong and weak points. Attack in an unsuspected manner, knowing his metre and modulation and the appropriate timing.

Knowing the times means, if your ability is high, seeing right into things. If you are thoroughly conversant with strategy, you will recognize the enemy's intentions and thus have many opportunities to win. You must sufficiently study this.

'To tread down the sword'

'To tread down the sword' is a principle often used in strategy. First, in large-scale strategy, when the enemy first discharges bows and guns and then attacks, it is difficult for us to attack if we are busy loading powder into our guns or notching our arrows. The spirit is to attack quickly while the enemy is still shooting with bows or guns. The spirit is to win by 'treading down' as we receive the enemy's attack.

In single combat, we cannot get a decisive victory by cutting, with a 'tee-dum, tee-dum' feeling, in the wake of the enemy's attacking long sword. We must defeat him at the start of his attack, in the spirit of treading him down with the feet, so that he cannot rise again to the attack.

'Treading' does not simply mean treading with the feet. Tread with the body, tread with the spirit, and, of course, tread and cut with the long sword. You must achieve the spirit of not allowing the enemy to attack a second time. This is the spirit of forestalling in every sense. Once at the enemy, you should not aspire just to strike him, but to cling after the attack. You must study this deeply.

To know 'collapse'

Everything can collapse. Houses, bodies, and enemies collapse when their rhythm becomes deranged.

In large-scale strategy, when the enemy starts to collapse, you must pursue him without letting the chance go. If you fail to take advantage of your enemies' collapse, they may recover.

In single combat, the enemy sometimes loses timing and collapses. If you let this opportunity pass, he may recover and not be so negligent thereafter. Fix your eye on the enemy's collapse, and chase him, attacking so that you do not let him recover. You must do this. The chasing attack is with a strong spirit. You must utterly cut the enemy down so that he does not recover his position. You must understand utterly how to cut down the enemy.

'To become the enemy'

'To become the enemy' means to think yourself into the enemy's position. In the world, people tend to think of a robber trapped in a house as a fortified enemy. However, if we think of 'becoming the enemy', we feel that the whole world is against us and that there is no escape. He who is shut inside is a pheasant. He who enters to arrest is a hawk. You must appreciate this.

In large-scale strategy, people are always under the impression that the enemy is strong, and so tend to become cautious. But if you have good soldiers, and if you understand the principles of strategy, and if you know how to beat the enemy, there is nothing to worry about.

In single combat, also, you must put yourself in the enemy's position. If you think, 'Here is a master of the Way, who knows the principles of strategy,' then you will surely lose. You must consider this deeply.

'To release four hands'

'To release four hands' is used when you and the enemy are contending with the same spirit, and the issue cannot be decided. Abandon this spirit and win through an alternative resource.

In large-scale strategy, when there is a 'four hands' spirit, do not give up – it is man's existence. Immediately throw away this spirit and win with a technique the enemy does not expect.

In single combat also, when we think we have fallen into the 'four hands' situation, we must defeat the enemy by changing our mind and applying a suitable technique according to his condition. You must be able to judge this.

'To move the shadow'

'To move the shadow' is used when you cannot see the enemy's spirit.

In large-scale strategy, when you cannot see the enemy's position, indicate that you are about to attack strongly, to discover his resources. It is easy then to defeat him with a different method once you see his resources.

In single combat, if the enemy takes up a rear or side attitude of the long sword so that you cannot see his intention, make a feint attack, and the enemy will show his long sword, thinking he sees your spirit. Benefiting from what you are shown, you can win with certainty. If you are negligent, you will miss the timing. Research this well.

'To hold down a shadow'

'Holding down a shadow' is used when you can see the enemy's attacking spirit.

In large-scale strategy, when the enemy embarks on an attack, if you make a show of strongly suppressing his technique, he will change his mind. Then, altering your spirit, defeat him by forestalling him with a Void spirit.

Or, in single combat, hold down the enemy's strong intention with a suitable timing, and defeat him by forestalling him with this timing. You must study this well.

• 111 •

To pass on

Many things are said to be passed on. Sleepiness can be passed on, and yawning can be passed on. Time can be passed on also.

In large-scale strategy, when the enemy is agitated and shows an inclination to rush, do not mind in the least. Make a show of complete calmness, and the enemy will be taken by this and will become relaxed. When you see that this spirit has been passed on, you can bring about the enemy's defeat by attacking strongly with a Void spirit.

In single combat, you can win by relaxing your body and spirit and then, catching on the moment the enemy relaxes, attack strongly and quickly, forestalling him.

What is known as 'getting someone drunk' is similar to this. You can also infect the enemy with a bored, careless, or weak spirit. You must study this well.

To cause loss of balance

Many things can cause a loss of balance. One cause is danger, another is hardship, and another is surprise. You must research this.

In large-scale strategy, it is important to cause loss of balance. Attack without warning where the enemy is not

expecting it, and while his spirit is undecided follow up your advantage and, having the lead, defeat him.

Or, in single combat, start by making a show of being slow, then suddenly attack strongly. Without allowing him space for breath to recover from the fluctuation of spirit, you must grasp the opportunity to win. Get the feel of this.

To frighten

Fright often occurs, caused by the unexpected.

In large-scale strategy, you can frighten the enemy not by what you present to their eyes, but by shouting, making a small force seem large, or by threatening them from the flank without warning. These things all frighten. You can win by making best use of the enemy's frightened rhythm.

In single combat, also, you must use the advantage of taking the enemy unawares by frightening him with your body, long sword, or voice, to defeat him. You should research this well.

'To soak in'

When you have come to grips, and are striving together with the enemy, and you realize that you cannot advance, you 'soak in' and become one with the enemy. You can win

by applying a suitable technique while you are mutually entangled.

In battles involving large numbers as well as in fights with small numbers, you can often win decisively with the advantage of knowing how to 'soak' into the enemy, whereas, were you to draw apart, you would lose the chance to win. Research this well.

'To injure the corners'

It is difficult to move strong things by pushing directly, so you should 'injure the corners'.

In large-scale strategy, it is beneficial to strike at the corners of the enemy's force. If the corners are overthrown, the spirit of the whole body will be overthrown. To defeat the enemy, you must follow up the attack when the corners have fallen.

In single combat, it is easy to win once the enemy collapses. This happens when you injure the 'corners' of his body, and this weakens him. It is important to know how to do this, so you must research it deeply.

To throw into confusion

This means making the enemy lose resolve.

In large-scale strategy, we can use our troops to confuse the enemy on the field. Observing the enemy's spirit, we can make him think, 'Here? There? Like that? Like this? Slow? Fast?' Victory is certain when the enemy is caught up in a rhythm that confuses his spirit.

In single combat, we can confuse the enemy by attacking with varied techniques when the chance arises. Feint a thrust or cut, or make the enemy think you are going close to him, and when he is confused you can easily win.

This is the essence of fighting, and you must research it deeply.

The Three Shouts

The Three Shouts are divided thus: before, during and after. Shout according to the situation. The voice is a thing of life. We shout against fires and so on, against the wind and the waves. The voice shows energy.

In large-scale strategy, at the start of battle we shout as loudly as possible. During the fight, the voice is low-pitched, shouting out as we attack. After the contest, we shout in the wake of our victory. These are the Three Shouts.

In single combat, we make as if to cut and shout 'Ei!' at the same time to disturb the enemy, then in the wake of our

shout we cut with the long sword. We shout after we have cut down the enemy – this is to announce victory. This is called 'sen go no koe' (before and after voice). We do not shout simultaneously with flourishing the long sword. We shout during the fight to get into rhythm. Research this deeply.

To mingle

In battles, when the armies are in confrontation, attack the enemy's strong points and, when you see that they are beaten back, quickly separate and attack yet another strong point on the periphery of his force. The spirit of this is like a winding mountain path.

This is an important fighting method for one man against many. Strike down the enemies in one quarter, or drive them back, then grasp the timing and attack further strong points to right and left, as if on a winding mountain path, weighing up the enemies' disposition. When you know the enemies' level, attack strongly with no trace of retreating spirit.

In single combat, too, use this spirit with the enemy's strong points.

What is meant by 'mingling' is the spirit of advancing and becoming engaged with the enemy, and not withdrawing even one step. You must understand this.

To crush

This means to crush the enemy, regarding him as being weak.

In large-scale strategy, when we see that the enemy has few men, or if he has many men but his spirit is weak and disordered, we knock the hat over his eyes, crushing him utterly. If we crush lightly, he may recover. You must learn the spirit of crushing as if with a hand-grip.

In single combat, if the enemy is less skilful than yourself, if his rhythm is disorganized, or if he has fallen into evasive

or retreating attitudes, we must crush him straightaway, with no concern for his presence and without allowing him space for breath. It is essential to crush him all at once. The primary thing is not to let him recover his position even a little. You must research this deeply.

The 'mountain-sea change'

The 'mountain-sea' spirit means that it is bad to repeat the same thing several times when fighting the enemy. There may be no help but to do something twice, but do not try it a third time. If you once make an attack and fail, there is little chance of success if you use the same approach again. If you attempt a technique which you have previously tried unsuccessfully and fail yet again, then you must change your attacking method.

If the enemy thinks of the mountains, attack like the sea; and if he thinks of the sea, attack like the mountains. You must research this deeply.

'To penetrate the depths'

When we are fighting with the enemy, even when it can be seen that we can win on the surface with the benefit of the Way, if his spirit is not extinguished, he may be beaten

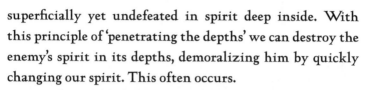

superficially yet undefeated in spirit deep inside. With this principle of 'penetrating the depths' we can destroy the enemy's spirit in its depths, demoralizing him by quickly changing our spirit. This often occurs.

Penetrating the depths means penetrating with the long sword, penetrating with the body, and penetrating with the spirit. This cannot be understood in a generalization.

Once we have crushed the enemy in the depths, there is no need to remain spirited. But otherwise we must remain spirited. If the enemy remains spirited, it is difficult to crush him. You must train in penetrating the depths for large-scale strategy and also single combat.

'To renew'

'To renew' applies when we are fighting with the enemy, and an entangled spirit arises where there is no possible resolution. We must abandon our efforts, think of the situation in a fresh spirit, then win in the new rhythm. To renew, when we are deadlocked with the enemy, means that without changing our circumstance we change our spirit and win through a different technique.

It is necessary to consider how 'to renew' also applies in large-scale strategy. Research this diligently.

'Rat's head, ox's neck'

'Rat's head, ox's neck' means that, when we are fighting with the enemy and both he and we have become occupied with small points in an entangled spirit, we must always think of the Way of strategy as being both a rat's head and an ox's neck. Whenever we have become preoccupied with small details, we must suddenly change into a large spirit, interchanging large with small.

This is one of the essences of strategy. It is necessary that the warrior think in this spirit in everyday life. You must not depart from this spirit in large-scale strategy nor in single combat.

'The commander knows the troops'

'The commander knows the troops' applies everywhere in fights in my Way of strategy.

Using the wisdom of strategy, think of the enemy as your own troops. When you think in this way, you can move him at will and be able to chase him around. You become the general and the enemy becomes your troops. You must master this.

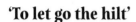

'To let go the hilt'

There are various kinds of spirit involved in letting go the hilt.

There is the spirit of winning without a sword. There is also the spirit of holding the long sword but not winning. The various methods cannot be expressed in writing. You must train well.

The 'body of a rock'

When you have mastered the Way of strategy, you can suddenly make your body like a rock, and ten thousand things cannot touch you. This is the 'body of a rock'.

Oral tradition: You will not be moved.

What is recorded above is what has been constantly on my mind about Ichi school sword-fencing, written down as it came to me. This is the first time I have written about my technique, and the order of things is a bit confused. It is difficult to express it clearly.

This book is a spiritual guide for the man who wishes to learn the Way.

My heart has been inclined to the Way of strategy from my youth onwards. I have devoted myself to training my hand, tempering my body, and attaining the many spiritual

attitudes of sword-fencing. If we watch men of other schools discussing theory, and concentrating on techniques with the hands, even though they seem skilful to watch, they have not the slightest true spirit.

Of course, men who study in this way think they are training the body and spirit, but it is an obstacle to the true Way, and its bad influence remains forever. Thus the true Way of strategy is becoming decadent and dying out.

The true Way of sword-fencing is the craft of defeating the enemy in a fight, and nothing other than this. If you attain and adhere to the wisdom of my strategy, you need never doubt that you will win.

TACTICS

'The Book of Fire' is concerned with battle tactics: of taking the initiative and dictating the course of events; of hoodwinking, wrongfooting and outperforming the enemy; of putting oneself in their shoes to discern their intentions while masking one's own. It has a profound application for those looking to get on in business, for it is essential to know one's competitors in order to stand out. This is especially true in the early days, when one is focused on getting a fledgling operation off the ground in what is almost certain to be a crowded space.

Musashi's messages are concerned with large-scale strategy as well as single combat, so can be used by entrepreneurs looking to overcome challenges both large and small.

Instil in Oneself the Spirit of Winning

He advocates for on-the-job training, as it is impossible to synthesize the focus that can only result from being subject to real world conditions and genuine threat. It is why he says, 'In my strategy, the training for killing enemies is by way of many contests, fighting for survival, discovering the meaning of life and death.'

And the more one trains with meaningful results, the greater the appetite one gets for success. Legendary US entrepreneur and co-founder of software company Oracle Corporation, Larry Ellison, knows this truth, as contained in his statement: 'I'm addicted to winning. The more you win, the more you want to win.' The martial arts film star Bruce Lee knew all too well the benefits of training when he said, 'Practice makes perfect. After a long time of practicing, our work will become natural, skillful, swift, and steady.' In dedicating himself to improvement, he was able to move from the backstreet gang culture of his youth to Hollywood stardom. Similarly, as Warren Buffett, the legendary investor widely recognized as the best stock picker in history, says: 'The best investment you can make is in yourself.'

Musashi is much concerned in 'The Book of Fire' with ways to crush the competition and proposes using all means at one's disposal and natural advantage. For example, he talks of 'using the virtues of the place to establish predominant positions from which to fight'. He also discusses affording no breathing space or time to regroup, and to turn the screw so that panic, chaos and confusion are amplified on the part of

the opposition. 'When the enemy gets into an inconvenient position, do not let him look around, but conscientiously chase him around and pin him down … not letting him see his situation,' he says.

At first sight, this sounds wholly ruthless and unnecessarily merciless to our contemporary senses, but there is something refreshingly authentic about Musashi's frank style. For all the warm notions about collaboration and compassion that mark the era we're living through, today's commercial arena remains a brutal and unforgiving place full of crocodile smiles. Musashi sought for his actions to be regulated and governed by a sense of honour, not the first thing one would associate with capitalism. The most successful entrepreneurs have always understood the rules of the game better than anyone else and have been prepared, unapologetically, to do what is necessary to get ahead.

Get Ahead of the Game

Facebook chief Mark Zuckerberg, for instance, managed to oust his co-founder Eduardo Saverin in the organization's early days so that he could assume a controlling stake in the company. Zuckerberg unleashed a series of stock manoeuvres that saw Saverin's stake diluted to the point of losing his right to be privy to decision-making and strategic direction. Saverin did not realize the magnitude of what had happened until it was too late.

Correspondence in the public domain indicates Zuckerberg's motivation for sidelining and removing Saverin

lay in a genuinely held belief that he was not up to the job, alongside a lack of shared vision. It is also probably true that, had Zuckerberg failed to neutralize Saverin, Facebook would not have turned into the all-conquering behemoth it became.

The route to disempowering Saverin, however, demanded Zuckerberg be wily, merciless and fearless of the lawsuits that were bound to come his way thereafter. For those wishing to prosper in spades, they must be comfortable with confrontation and grasp the fact that people-pleasing is always the enemy of success. According to Musashi, 'If you let this opportunity pass, he may recover and not be so negligent thereafter. You must utterly cut the enemy down so that he does not recover his position.'

'The Book of Fire' also points to the importance of making use of geography. Zuckerberg moved operations to Palo Alto, California, dropping out of Harvard to avail himself of the Silicon Valley pool of talent and tech investor community that would be on his doorstep. This afforded him an advantage over his co-founder, Saverin, who remained on the east coast with an internship at Lehman Brothers in New York. In Musashi's words, from California, Zuckerberg was able to use 'the virtues of the place to establish predominant positions from which to fight'.

The attacking method Zuckerberg used to establish effective autonomy over Facebook is what Musashi would call *Ken No Sen*, one of the three ways he describes by which the enemy can be forestalled. Zuckerberg followed exactly Musashi's direction that, 'When you decide to attack, keep

calm and dash in quickly,' and remained unmoved by Saverin's protests, embodying *The Book of Five Rings*' instruction: 'With your spirit calm, attack with a feeling of constantly crushing the enemy, from first to last.'

The second method Musashi communicates is known as *Tai No Sen*. This can involve feigning weakness and can be a highly effective strategy for manipulating or exploiting others to achieve one's ends. It serves to lull the competition into a false sense of security and causes them to be careless and sloppy, letting their guard down to reveal their intent.

A great example of this is Vladimir Putin, President of Russia, who ceaselessly gives false hope to his enemies in the West that his regime is on the ropes or that he himself is in poor health, or even mortally ill. It is a classic example of confirmation bias being used to infer something without any firm evidence, simply because there is such a strong appetite for it to be true. Putin also appears to have deployed this approach when Yevgeny Prigozhin marched his Wagner Group of mercenaries towards Moscow in protest at the Russian government's inept handling of Russia's 'Special Military Operation in Ukraine' – an operation Prigozhin claimed was exposing his men to unnecessary risk. This blatant challenge to Putin's authority was met at the time with what appeared to be a muted and weak response from the Russian leader that seemingly allowed Prigozhin to stand down without any consequences. Yet, within a matter of weeks, the mercenary leader was dead, killed in a mysterious plane crash along with a number of his acolytes.

Putin, from the mean Cold War streets of St Petersburg, is the classic clinical entrepreneur, working his way up through the ranks of the KGB/FSB to become leader of the world's largest country, using every means available to him to crush the opposition and cement his authority against every pretender to his crown. Effective, but decidedly lacking in honour. Not Musashi's sort of warrior.

Musashi also describes a third way of forestalling the enemy, what he calls *Tai Tai No Sen*, which involves meeting like with like. So, for example, when the Socialist Party mayor of Paris Anne Hidalgo was in dire need of a popular cause to be aligned with in order to boost her waning popularity with voters, she struck on the evils of e-scooters as the perfect (or imperfect) vehicle. This saw her tapping into fears regarding the health and safety dangers the e-scooter presented for Parisians and engineering a binding referendum in April 2023 regarding their continued use. Most e-scooter users are young, a demographic known to stay away from the polling booth. Predictably, they did not turn out in sufficient numbers to provide an accurate reflection of public sentiment. This left the playing field open to older and more conservative-minded voters, people who traditionally fear change and who in this case saw the new modes of transport as a menace.

Conflict is Good. Avoid Avoiding it

We are also told by Musashi that we must not be afraid of locking horns. Conflict is inevitable in commerce today, just as it was for the warrior in his time. Attempting to avoid

engagement and keep one's head below the parapet is only an option for entrepreneurs with nothing of value or substance to offer; if that which you have is deemed to constitute a threat to the competition, sooner or later they will seek you out and come for you, even when you have done your best not to court conflict. There is nothing dishonourable about being on the front foot is the message here. Seize the day and take the initiative, intimates Musashi, as illustrated when he says that, 'In contests of strategy, it is bad to be led about by the enemy. You must always be able to lead the enemy about.' Conversely, it makes sense to keep the competitors on the back foot, since they 'cannot forestall you if you do not allow [them] to come out'.

This involves anticipating their course of action and putting measures in place to nip it in the bud, so that they get no traction. As Musashi details: 'whatever the enemy tries to bring about in the fight you will see in advance and suppress it … suppress the enemy's techniques, foil his plans and thence command him directly.'

If one doesn't let the competition get out of the starting blocks, their ambitions will be frustrated, gaining for oneself valuable time to get ahead or better prepare for a day of reckoning further down the line. Many incumbents use the law to keep upstarts down, while being cognisant of anti-trust legislation designed to protect and promote competition, and to prevent collusion and monopolies from taking hold. Tactics can include aggressively defending intellectual property rights or appealing to the government of the day

to act. Entrepreneurs should not be deterred, however. Even the most determined and unified campaigns by incumbents, while sometimes slowing down the introduction of new disruptive products or services, are only serving to delay the inevitable if that which they seek to keep out answers a need they are failing to meet. If an innovation is good enough and has backing, traction and visibility, it cannot be kept down indefinitely.

Think of the concerted but generally unsuccessful campaigns across major global cities by taxi drivers to stop the app-based Uber service from shaking things up, or of the established record industry suing music streaming services, such as Spotify, claiming copyright infringement. Both are now firmly established market players. Or put oneself in mind of big oil's doomed offensive against the introduction of electric vehicles.

Even when forces are ranged against them, the true entrepreneur is determined, resolute and confident enough in what they have to meet those forces head on. There is no way to discover what limits there are to what can be achieved if one hides away, shies away from a challenge, or lets others walk all over them. Oracle's Larry Ellison has been quoted as saying that 'Life's a journey. It's a journey about discovering limits,' and 'All you can do is all you can do.'

When all that can be done to create the internal conditions for success has been done and the external conditions are set fair, the time is as opportune to venture into the market-place as it will ever be. As Musashi said: 'It means setting

sail even though your friends stay in harbour, knowing the route, knowing the soundness of your ship and the favour of the day. When all the conditions are met, and there is perhaps a favourable wind, or a tailwind, then set sail.' At the same time, it is essential to play to one's strengths – be that what one offers is cheaper, faster, stronger or any other of the myriad indicators of 'better' – and focus on the differentiator to distinguish oneself from and elevate oneself above the competition. It is how to apply Musashi's wisdom encapsulated in his words: 'knowing your own strong points, "cross the ford" at the advantageous place … If you succeed in crossing at the best place, you may take your ease.'

This knowledge of where to strike and what to shout about is as important for sole traders seeking to gain a foothold in the local economy as it is for ventures with multi-million-dollar backing looking to release upon the world a society-changing innovation. According to Musashi: 'The spirit of crossing at a ford is necessary in both large- and small-scale strategy.'

Forever Focused

The Greek philosopher Heraclitus mused that, 'The only constant in life is change.' He also asserted that, 'You cannot step in the same river twice.' Musashi echoes these enduring and entrepreneur-friendly sentiments throughout *The Book of Five Rings* and in 'The Book of Fire' gives the modern-day businessperson much to think about when he says that one must 'know the times' and determine whether the enemy is 'flourishing or waning'.

Successful bright young companies mature, and those overseeing the initial success often become complacent and stop innovating – perhaps focusing instead on the spoils of their success. Alternatively, new personnel brought in can lack the zeal of the founders. This can lead to slow decline.

Such decline may not find form in a loss of market share or falling profits at first, but in taking their eye off the ball, stopping learning, or thinking they've made it and are untouchable, the entrepreneur that drove that initial success may stop behaving as an entrepreneur should, thus placing their company at risk.

Corporate history is littered with examples of companies in a state of stagnation or those engaged in self-approbation. Amazon's Jeff Bezos recognizes this and it is why he espouses the 'Day One' philosophy, to stay constantly focused and motivated. He explained it thus in a letter to shareholders in 2016: 'Day 2 is stasis. Followed by irrelevance. Followed by excruciating, painful decline. Followed by death. And that is why it is always Day 1.' Those not adhering to Bezos' advice constitute golden opportunities for bright young things to muscle in and make their mark with an alternative that sits in marked and positive contrast to the established offer.

Apple is one example of a firm that understood 'the enemy's disposition', as Musashi would see it. What co-founder of Apple Inc. Steve Jobs saw was the lumbering nature of big business. As a lifelong practitioner of Zen meditation on the back of a lengthy trip to India in his late teens, Jobs' unconventional spiritual approach to commerce allowed him to see past

the usual customs and conventions of business to believe that things could be done differently. More specifically, the brief he gave himself and those around him was to create a personal computer that was affordable, user friendly and had more power, since what currently existed was none of those things. Apple fulfilled the brief to much acclaim and success. The ardour Jobs' brand of entrepreneurialism was marked by broke the mould and carried through into the Apple products he oversaw, not least the first iPhone in 2007, a multimedia touch-screen smartphone that revolutionized the mobile phone market and left the competition reeling.

'Knowing the times means, if your ability is high, seeing right into things,' says Musashi. Steve Jobs was one of the all-time great entrepreneurs who saw into things more than most.

You are not an Impostor

One of the most interesting passages in *The Book of Five Rings* sees Musashi warn the reader not to overestimate the enemy, contrary to the expected note of caution not to underestimate them. Over-confidence is bad, but confidence rooted in reality is good, for as Musashi explains, 'people are always under the impression that the enemy is strong, and so tend to become cautious. But if you have good soldiers, and if you understand the principles of strategy, and if you know how to beat the enemy, there is nothing to worry about.'

Those looking to get on in business today can take from this that they should avoid becoming over-humble, giving the competition undeserved credence or succumbing to

impostor syndrome, since this can lead to one becoming indecisive and to an inert paralyzed business that will fail to fulfil its potential. 'If you think, "Here is a master of the Way, who knows the principles of strategy," then you will surely lose,' says Musashi.

Be Hungry for Change

The positive power of change is reinforced by Musashi pointing out that when you mix it up to break an impasse, the chances of victory increase. Sometimes in business, the status quo has existed for so long you can lead the competition to believe you are content with them doing their thing and you yours in perpetuity. However, such a state of permanence runs contrary to the laws of commerce. If one's competitors mistake one's honour for apathy or an aversion towards rivalry and become too relaxed, it is exclusively on them when a rival takes advantage of the opportunity they have gifted and moves in on their market patch. As Musashi says: 'You can … infect the enemy with a bored, careless, or weak spirit.'

In business, if all of the players keep doing the same thing, the best that can be hoped for is an uneasy coexistence and a predictable stagnant market where the consumer is short-changed of value. Price-fixing cartels are one such example that stifle the incentivization to be better.

Competition breeds excellence and, quite apart from the benefits to a business and its stakeholders that comes from using a different technique to secure advantage, it

will also spur competitors on to up their game, which is the bedrock of commerce. As Bill Gates, co-founder of software giant, Microsoft says: 'Whether it's Google or Apple or free software, we've got some fantastic competitors and it keeps us on our toes.'

Impressions are important. If one can impress upon multiple targets in coordinated fashion and using all channels the absolute confidence one has in oneself, one's team, and the capacity of one's product or service to scratch a market itch, investors and consumers alike will become swiftly convinced. Moreover, the competition will be wowed, intimidated and lose morale from the noise one makes and at the thought of what's to come, and will be more likely to submit or share market space without putting up much resistance. Musashi refers to it as 'frightening the enemy'. He notes that, 'You can frighten the enemy not by what you present to their eyes, but by shouting, making a small force seem large, or by threatening them from the flank without warning.'

Varying one's tactics to avoid predictability and bamboozle and confuse the opposition is something Musashi held dear. 'Observing the enemy's spirit, we can make him think, "Here? There? Like that? Like this? Slow? Fast?"', he says.

These diversified tactics can still adhere to the overall strategic objective. In fact, proper execution of a strategy should be marked by the use of a variety of techniques. As Canadian academic and author Henry Mintzberg notes: 'Strategy is a pattern in a stream of decisions.'

It is certainly the case that if one keeps deploying the same tactics progress will be hard to make, since one is locked into a cycle of repeat. Competitors will know exactly what to expect and be able to navigate and bat away the challenge with ease. No less a figure than Albert Einstein understood this when he observed that, 'If you always do what you always did, you will always get what you always got.'

Entrepreneurs take note: the greatest minds in history advocate mixing things up to optimize the chances of success. Doing the unexpected is an extremely potent way of operating, and just as Austrian-born Arnold Schwarzenegger started from humble beginnings to wear many different and brilliant hats in his lifetime to great acclaim – bodybuilder, film star and politician – so too can anyone else if they orient themselves to change. It is just as Musashi says: 'If the enemy thinks of the mountains, attack like the sea; and if he thinks of the sea, attack like the mountains.'

Equally, when the prospect of victory is receding or the resolution of a problem is unreachable, one must be honest with oneself and admit the approach being used is not working. The best entrepreneurs recognize when it is time to come at a challenge from a different place. Musashi calls it 'to renew' and instructs that 'we change our spirit and win through a different technique'.

Big Picture Passion and Zeal

And when victory is achieved – while being mindful that you are only as good as your last fight, sale or deal and should not

become vainglorious – take time to let the world know about it. Just as it was for the warrior in Musashi's time, your victory is good news for you and your business, will serve to bolster your credentials in the eyes of others and will attach to you the aura of success. This will mean competitors are warier of you and customers will come flocking. With the advent of multiple communication conduits there are now almost infinite ways to broadcast your achievements. Musashi says not to hold back: 'We shout after we have cut down the enemy – this is to announce victory.'

Never lose sight of the big picture is also one of Musashi's key messages from 'The Book of Fire'. Tactics deployed must be subordinate to the overall objective, which should itself be simple. For Musashi, it was to defeat the enemy and prevail. Entrepreneurs must leave the fine minutiae of operations to others and resist the temptation to micromanage. 'Whenever we have become preoccupied with small details, we must suddenly change into a large spirit, interchanging large with small,' says Musashi.

This is as true today as it was then for those wishing to make headway. Steve Jobs and Jeff Bezos both agree on this point. According to Jobs: 'It doesn't make sense to hire smart people and tell them what to do; we hire smart people so they can tell us what to do.' For Bezos, 'Micromanagement is the enemy of innovation.'

CHAPTER FOUR

THE BOOK OF WIND

Original Text

In strategy, you must know the Ways of other schools, so I have written about various other traditions of strategy in this, the Book of Wind.

Without knowledge of the Ways of other schools, it is difficult to understand the essence of my Ichi school. Looking at other schools we find some that specialize in techniques of strength using extra-long swords. Some schools study the Way of the short sword, known as 'kodachi'. Some schools teach dexterity in large numbers of sword techniques, teaching attitudes of the sword as the 'surface' and the Way as the 'interior'.

That none of these are the true Way I show clearly in the interior of this book – all the vices and virtues and rights and wrongs. My Ichi school is different. Other schools make accomplishments their means of livelihood, growing flowers and decoratively colouring articles in order to sell them. This is definitely not the Way of strategy.

Some of the world's strategists are concerned only with sword-fencing, and limit their training to flourishing the long sword and carriage of the body. But is dexterity alone sufficient to win? This is not the essence of the Way.

I have recorded the unsatisfactory points of other schools one by one in this book. You must study these matters deeply to appreciate the benefit of my Nito Ichi school.

Other schools using extra-long swords

Some other schools have a liking for extra-long swords. From the point of view of my strategy, these must be seen as weak schools. This is because they do not appreciate the principle of cutting the enemy by any means. Their preference is for

the extra-long sword and, relying on the virtue of its length, they think to defeat the enemy from a distance.

In this world it is said, 'One inch gives the hand advantage,' but these are the idle words of one who does not know strategy. It shows the inferior strategy of a weak spirit that men should be dependent on the length of their sword, fighting from a distance without the benefit of strategy.

I expect there is a case for the school in question liking extra-long swords as part of its doctrine, but if we compare this with real life it is unreasonable. Surely, we need not necessarily be defeated if we are using a short sword and have no long sword?

It is difficult for these people to cut the enemy when at close quarters because of the length of the long sword. The blade path is large so the long sword is an encumbrance, and they are at a disadvantage compared to the man armed with a short companion sword.

From olden times it has been said: 'Great and small go together.' So do not unconditionally dislike extra-long swords. What I dislike is the inclination towards the long sword. If we consider large-scale strategy, we can think of large forces in terms of long swords, and small forces as short swords. Cannot few men give battle against many?

There are many instances of few men overcoming many.

Your strategy is of no account if, when called on to fight in a confined space, your heart is inclined to the long sword, or if you are in a house armed only with your companion sword. Besides, some men have not the strength of others.

In my doctrine, I dislike preconceived, narrow spirit. You must study this well.

The strong long sword spirit in other schools

You should not speak of strong and weak long swords. If you just wield the long sword in a strong spirit your cutting will become coarse, and if you use the sword coarsely you will have difficulty in winning.

If you are concerned with the strength of your sword, you will try to cut unreasonably strongly, and will not be able to cut at all. It is also bad to try to cut strongly when testing the sword. Whenever you cross swords with an enemy you must not think of cutting him either strongly or weakly; just think of cutting and killing him. Be intent solely on killing the enemy. Do not try to cut strongly and, of course, do not think of cutting weakly. You should only be concerned with killing the enemy.

If you rely on strength, when you hit the enemy's sword you will inevitably hit too hard. If you do this, your own sword will be carried along as a result. Thus, the saying, 'the strongest hand wins', has no meaning.

In large-scale strategy, if you have a strong army and are relying on strength to win but the enemy also has a strong army, the battle will be fierce. This is the same for both sides.

Without the correct principle, the fight cannot be won.

The spirit of my school is to win through the wisdom of strategy, paying no attention to trifles. Study this well.

Use of the shorter long sword in other schools

Using a shorter long sword is not the true Way to win.

In ancient times, 'tachi' and 'katana' meant long and short swords. Men of superior strength in the world can wield even a long sword lightly, so there is no case for their liking the short sword. They also make use of the length of spears and halberds. Some men use a shorter long sword with the intention of jumping in and stabbing the enemy at the unguarded moment when he flourishes his sword. This inclination is bad.

To aim for the enemy's unguarded moment is completely defensive, and undesirable at close quarters with the enemy.

Furthermore, you cannot use the method of jumping inside his defence with a short sword if there are many enemies. Some men think that if they go against many enemies with a shorter long sword they can unrestrictedly frisk around cutting in sweeps, but they have to parry cuts continuously, and eventually become entangled with the enemy. This is inconsistent with the true Way of strategy.

The sure Way to win thus is to chase the enemy around in a confusing manner, causing him to jump aside, with your body held strongly and straight. The same principle applies to large-scale strategy. The essence of strategy is to fall upon the enemy in large numbers and to bring about his speedy downfall. By their study of strategy, people of the world get used to countering, evading and retreating as the normal thing. They become set in this habit, so can easily be paraded around by the enemy. The Way of strategy is straight and true. You must chase the enemy around and make him obey your spirit.

Other schools with many methods of using the long sword

I think it is held in other schools that there are many ways of using the longsword in order to gain the admiration

of beginners; this is selling the Way. It is a vile Spirit in strategy. The reason for this is that to deliberate over many ways of cutting down a man is an error.

To start with, killing is not the way of mankind. Killing is the same for women or children and there are not many methods. We can speak of tactics such as stabbing and mowing down but none other than these. Anyway, cutting down an enemy is the way of strategy and there is no need for many refinements of it,

Even so, according to the place obstructed above or to the sides and you will need to hold your sword in such a manner that it can be used. There are five methods in five directions. Methods apart from these five, hand twisting, body bending, jumping out and so on to cut the enemy are not the true way of strategy.

In order to cut the enemy you must not make twisting or bending cuts. This is completely useless. In my strategy I bear my spirit and body straight and cause the enemy to twist and bend.

The necessary Spirit is to win by attacking the enemy when his Spirit is warped. You must study this well.

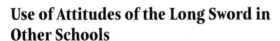

Use of Attitudes of the Long Sword in Other Schools

Placing a great deal of importance on the attitudes of the long sword is a mistaken way of thinking. What is known in the world as 'attitude' applies when there is no enemy. The reason is that this has been a precedent since ancient times, and there should be no such thing as 'This is the modern way to do it' in duelling. You must force the enemy into inconvenient situations.

Attitudes are for situations in which you are not to be moved. That is, for garrisoning castles, battle array, and so on, showing the spirit of not being moved even by a strong assault. In the Way of duelling, however, you must always be intent upon taking the lead and attacking. Attitude is the spirit of awaiting an attack. You must appreciate this.

In duels of strategy you must move the opponent's attitude. Attack where his spirit is lax, throw him into confusion, irritate and terrify him. Take advantage of the enemy's rhythm when he is unsettled and you can win.

I dislike the defensive spirit known as 'attitude'. Therefore, in my Way, there is something called 'Attitude-No-Attitude'.

In large-scale strategy, we deploy our troops for battle bearing in mind our strength, observing the enemy's numbers, and noting the details of the battlefield. This is at the start of the battle.

The spirit of attacking is completely different from the spirit of being attacked. Bearing an attack well, with a strong attitude, and parrying the enemy's attack well, is like making a wall of spears and halberds. When you attack the enemy, your spirit must go to the extent of pulling the stakes out of a wall and using them as spears and halberds. You must examine this well.

Fixing the eyes in other schools

Some schools maintain that the eyes should be fixed on the enemy's long sword. Some schools fix the eyes on the hands. Some fix the eyes on the face, and some fix the eyes on the feet, and so on. If you fix the eyes on these places, your spirit can become confused and your strategy thwarted.

I will explain this in detail. Footballers do not fix their eyes on the ball, but by good play on the field they can perform well. When you become accustomed to something, you are not limited to the use of your eyes. People such as master musicians have the music score in front of their

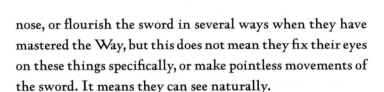

nose, or flourish the sword in several ways when they have mastered the Way, but this does not mean they fix their eyes on these things specifically, or make pointless movements of the sword. It means they can see naturally.

In the Way of strategy, when you have fought many times you will easily be able to appraise the speed and position of the enemy's sword, and having mastery of the Way you will see the weight of his spirit. In strategy, fixing the eyes means gazing at the man's heart.

In large-scale strategy, the area to watch is the enemy's strength. 'Perception' and 'sight' are the two methods of seeing. Perception consists of concentrating strongly on the enemy's spirit, observing the condition of the battlefield, fixing the gaze strongly, seeing the progress of the fight and the changes of advantage. This is the sure way to win.

In single combat, you must not fix the eyes on details. As I said before, if you fix your eyes on details and neglect important things, your spirit will become bewildered, and victory will escape you. Research this principle well and train diligently.

Use of the feet in other schools

There are various methods of using the feet: floating foot, jumping foot, springing foot, treading foot, crow's foot, and

such nimble walking methods. From the point of view of my strategy, these are all unsatisfactory.

I dislike floating foot because the feet always tend to float during the fight. The Way must be trod firmly.

Neither do I like jumping foot, because it encourages the habit of jumping, and a jumpy spirit. However much you jump, there is no real justification for it, so jumping is bad.

Springing foot causes a springing spirit which is indecisive.

Treading foot is a 'waiting' method, and I especially dislike it.

Apart from these, there are various fast walking methods, such as crow's foot, and so on.

Sometimes, however, you may encounter the enemy on marshland, swampy ground, river valleys, stony ground, or narrow roads, in which situations you cannot jump or move the feet quickly.

In my strategy, the footwork does not change. I always walk as I usually do in the street. You must never lose control of your feet. According to the enemy's rhythm, move fast or slowly, adjusting your body not too much and not too little.

Carrying the feet is important also in large-scale strategy. This is because, if you attack quickly and thoughtlessly without knowing the enemy's spirit, your rhythm will become

deranged and you will not be able to win. Or, if you advance too slowly, you will not be able to take advantage of the enemy's disorder, the opportunity to win will escape, and you will not be able to finish the fight quickly. You must win by seizing upon the enemy's disorder and derangement, and by not according him even a little hope of recovery. Practise this well.

Speed in other schools

Speed is not part of the true Way of strategy. Speed implies that things seem fast or slow, according to whether or not they are in rhythm. Whatever the Way, the master of strategy does not appear fast.

Some people can walk as fast as a hundred or a hundred and twenty miles in a day, but this does not mean that they run continuously from morning till night. Unpractised runners may seem to have been running all day, but their performance is poor.

In the Way of dance, accomplished performers can sing while dancing, but when beginners try this they slow down and their spirit becomes busy. The 'old pine tree' melody beaten on a leather drum is tranquil, but when beginners try this they slow down and their spirit becomes busy. Very skilful people can manage a fast rhythm, but it is bad to beat

hurriedly. If you try to beat too quickly you will get out of time. Of course, slowness is bad. Really skilful people never get out of time, and are always deliberate, and never appear busy. From this example, the principle can be seen.

What is known as speed is especially bad in the Way of strategy. The reason for this is that depending on the place, marsh or swamp and so on, it may not be possible to move the body and legs together quickly. Still less will you be able to cut quickly if you have a long sword in this situation. If you try to cut quickly, as if using a fan or short sword, you will not actually cut even a little. You must appreciate this.

In large-scale strategy also, a fast, busy spirit is undesirable. The spirit must be that of 'holding down a pillow', then you will not be even a little late.

When your opponent is hurrying recklessly, you must act contrarily, and keep calm. You must not be influenced by the opponent. Train diligently to attain this spirit.

'Interior' and 'surface' in other schools

There is no 'interior' nor 'surface' in strategy. The artistic accomplishments usually claim inner meaning and secret tradition, and 'interior' and 'gate' but in combat there is no such thing as fighting on the surface, or cutting with the

interior. When I teach my Way, I first teach by training in techniques which are easy for the pupil to understand, a doctrine which is easy to understand. I gradually endeavour to explain the deep principle, points which it is hardly possible to comprehend, according to the pupil's progress. In any event, because the way to understanding is through experience, I do not speak of 'interior' and 'gate'.

In this world, if you go into the mountains, and decide to go deeper and yet deeper, instead you will emerge at the gate. Whatever is the Way, it has an interior, and it is sometimes a good thing to point out the gate. In strategy, we cannot say what is concealed and what is revealed.

Accordingly, I dislike passing on my Way through written pledges and regulations. Perceiving the ability of my pupils, I teach the direct Way, remove the bad influence of other schools, and gradually introduce them to the true Way of the warrior.

The method of teaching my strategy is with a trustworthy spirit. You must train diligently.

I have tried to record an outline of the strategy of other schools in the above nine sections.

I could now continue by giving a specific account of these schools one by one, from the 'gate' to the 'interior', but I have

intentionally not named the schools or their main points.

The reason for this is that different branches of schools give different interpretations of the doctrines. In as much as men's opinions differ, so there must be differing ideas on the same matter. Thus no one man's conception is valid for any school.

I have shown the general tendencies of other schools on nine points. If we look at them from an honest viewpoint, we see that people always tend to like long swords or short swords, and become concerned with strength in both large and small matters. You can see why I do not deal with the 'gates' of other schools.

In my Ichi school of the long sword there is neither gate nor interior. There is no inner meaning in sword attitudes. You must simply keep your spirit true to realize the virtue of strategy.

SUBSTANCE OVER STYLE

The underlying message of 'The Book of Wind' is that, while it is essential to know oneself, one is not an island. To prosper, one must seek to understand the rationales, motivations and drives of others.

For Musashi, this was to better determine what to expect from an opponent in a duel, providing valuable insights on how best to prevail. And for today's entrepreneur it is about walking in someone else's shoes. This is about understanding what the competition is doing and why, in order to position one's own offer accordingly.

This seeing of things from another perspective can and should be extended to encompass all stakeholders: one's own team, suppliers, investors, regulators, and consumers

connected with one's proposition. All such groups have the power to make or break, and while they are not 'opponents' as Musashi would see them, their behaviours demand investigation if one wants to prosper.

Musashi the Salesman

At first read, 'The Book of Wind' comes across as a bit of a sales pitch by Musashi for his *Nito Ichi* school, whereby he denigrates the other martial arts as flawed, insubstantial and fleeting (like the wind) and, ultimately, inferior, compared to the true Way he claims to afford access to.

By today's standards, the chapter lacks grace and subtlety, with Musashi coming across as rather arrogant. His repeated disparaging remarks even go so far as to suggest he's not entirely convinced by his own rhetoric. If he is so sure of the superiority of what he advocates, why not let his school speak for itself and resist the temptation to run down the competition? After all, he has the pedigree and the credentials, having an unblemished duelling record across 61 encounters.

His main bugbears regarding other schools are that they are one-dimensional, prescriptive and obsessed with status. This contrasts with his, which he positions as being rooted in reality and rationality, and which teaches the merits of flexibility and adaptability to be able to respond to any number of different encounters.

We note anger and fastidiousness in how Musashi views these other schools, and he comes across as super-earnest, with an energy that is intense rather than ebullient. This is

because he is trying to impress on the reader that if you do not take his words seriously and apply them holistically, rather than selecting this or that part and rejecting others, it will be impossible to absorb his meaning and could mean the difference between life and death. And so too could the entrepreneur's fortunes rest on truly onboarding and applying his mindset of success while sounding out the spin and hyperbole.

In response to his rallying cry to have a diversified 'jack-of-all-trades' skill set, there are those that would argue specialization is no bad thing and speaks to expertise in a particular discipline. Warren Buffett, for example, says that 'Diversification is protection against ignorance. It makes little sense if you know what you are doing.' The native Nebraskan who heads up the conglomerate Berkshire Hathaway is famous for outsized returns on his investments, and there are many who seek to ape his moves and strategies, hoping for reflected glory with quantifiable benefits.

It would be hard to make a case for the concentrated investment strategy Buffett and his firm have been synonymous with over the years being a failure. Musashi, however, mocks other martial arts schools for prioritizing making a living when he says that, 'Other schools make accomplishments their means of livelihood ... This is definitely not the Way of strategy.'

Today, winning for entrepreneurs demands that revenues and profits are not trifling matters, but rather concerns of the utmost importance. In other words, survival before honour.

Musashi says that, 'It shows the inferior strategy of a weak spirit that men should be dependent on the length of their sword, fighting from a distance without the benefit of strategy.' His firm rejection of the exclusive use of extra-long swords comes from his belief that attempting to engage in combat from a distance is not only futile but counter-productive, since one is too far removed from the action to strike properly or decisively. Similarly, in business, especially in the early stages, an entrepreneur needs to be in the thick of it, getting their hands dirty to gain a sense of which aspects of the business are going well and which need addressing.

Keep it Simple and Block Out the Noise

Musashi is also keen that his audience focus on optimized actions as opposed to those informed by what is in vogue. It is why he remarks that, 'There should be no such thing as "This is the modern way to do it"' in duelling. This epitomizes the message of substance over style that underpins 'The Book of Wind', where all that matters is inconveniencing the opposition so that their threat is neutralized. For Musashi, that could mean injuring or killing the opponent; for today's less pugilistic-minded entrepreneur, it could relate to clearing a target market area of competitors. Either way, there's a peerless way of doing these things. Musashi thinks he knows what it is, but what is certain is that it rarely has anything to do with what others are doing.

Musashi advocates for agitating the enemy, believing that if one ruffles their feathers they are likely to lose focus and

expose their weaknesses. 'Attack where his spirit is lax, throw him into confusion, irritate and terrify him. Take advantage of the enemy's rhythm when he is unsettled and you can win,' he says.

As to whether Musashi's logic has application for entrepreneurs today to secure competitive advantage, many would disagree. Among those are Jeff Bezos, who says that, 'If you're competitor focused, you have to wait until there is a competitor doing something.'

It is better not to become fixated on detail, Musashi reminds the reader, when he says: 'If you fix your eyes on details and neglect important things, your spirit will become bewildered, and victory will escape you.' Those that focus only on what is in front of their face cannot spot what's looming on the horizon, and he uses the example of 'master musicians [who] have the music score in front of their nose … but this does not mean they fix their eyes on these things specifically'.

The jury seems to be out on the merits or otherwise of paying attention to detail, but perhaps founder of Twitter, Jack Dorsey, sums up the ideal path to pursue when he advises that we should 'Make every detail perfect and limit the number of details to perfect.'

Managing Minds

For entrepreneurs, giving off the appearance of effortlessness can be very useful in attracting publicity for their endeavours, with interested parties marvelling at the apparent ease with

which success comes to them and wanting to be in the orbit of that winning mentality. An even temperament not prone to rashness or impulsiveness will assist here, since people are reassured by those that appear unflappable, believing them to be in control of a situation when others are losing their heads. They will lend their support to and want to follow those with such an air of self-possession.

So long as one keeps in mind that this is an illusion and that what truly lies behind success is hard graft, it is fine to let others believe in one's preordained good fortune. It will act to draw in finance, contracts, talent and at the same time unsettle the competition. Rivals will believe perhaps that you are stronger and more powerful than you are and keep their distance, or make ill-informed strategic moves in response – all of which are good things. As Musashi says: 'Really skilful people never get out of time, and are always deliberate, and never appear busy.'

Even if it looks as though someone's ascendancy has been serene and effortless, that is usually not the case. Alternatively, access to the top table has been gifted to them on the back of someone else's entrepreneurship. So, in fact, they've achieved very little, and having missed out on the all-important learning curve will have nothing to draw on in the face of adversity. 'The way to understanding is through experience,' says Musashi.

Such individuals most likely also have issues regarding self-worth and entitlement, since they haven't earned their stripes and know it deep down. Former British Prime Minister,

Margaret Thatcher, understood it. 'I do not know anyone who has got to the top without hard work. That is the recipe. It will not always get you to the top, but should get you pretty near,' she said. Steve Jobs agreed. 'If you look really closely, most overnight successes took a long time,' he once said.

Keeping it Real

Rather than focusing on the enemy's weapon, focus on them, Musashi tells us, and we can glean from this that sometimes there is no substitute for face-to-face engagement. It is why executives and politicians criss-cross the world for in-person meetings. Being in the physical presence of someone affords an insight into their temperament, state of mind, intentions, convictions and how authentic they are in a way that remote video conferencing can't hope to replicate. It is much harder to fake it in person. Musashi knew how important it was to see the whites of someone's eyes when he said that, 'Perception consists of concentrating strongly on the enemy's spirit, observing the condition of the battlefield, fixing the gaze strongly, seeing the progress of the fight and the changes of advantages.'

Prioritizing social media contact over real world engagement to assess the true lay of the land is madness, since everyone in the digital world is curating their content to present a very controlled version of themselves or whatever thing they are tasked with promoting. Entrepreneur and three-time New York mayor Mike Bloomberg spoke of this in his 2021 speech at Johns Hopkins University, when lockdown

restrictions were being lifted – a situation that gave his words additional resonance when he declared that, 'There is real power in getting people together in person.'

Musashi concludes 'The Book of Wind' by warning the reader not to become obsessed by searching for hidden meaning in things. 'In combat there is no such thing as fighting on the surface, or cutting with the interior,' he says. For him, it is not about the superficial and the soulful existing as two separate planes; rather, they exist together as one, and through training a person will be able to understand the interconnectedness of things and comprehend the macro and micro forces in parallel. This is the holy grail, and those most predisposed to entrepreneurship will possess this capacity in raw unrefined form at the outset of their journey.

Keep it simple, be present and exercise mindfulness is Musashi's message that reaches out across the centuries, and his nirvanic take on life is encapsulated in the final words of 'The Book of Wind': 'There is no inner meaning in sword attitudes. You must simply keep your spirit true to realize the virtue of strategy.'

CHAPTER
FIVE

THE BOOK
OF THE VOID

Original Text

The Nito Ichi Way of strategy is recorded in this, the Book of the Void. What is called the spirit of the void is where there is nothing. It is not included in man's knowledge. Of course, the void is nothingness. By knowing things that exist, you can know that which does not exist. That is the void.

People in this world look at things mistakenly, and think that what they do not understand must be the void. This is not the true void. It is bewilderment.

In the Way of strategy, also, those who study as warriors think that whatever they cannot understand in their craft is the void. This is not the true void.

To attain the Way of strategy as a warrior, you must study fully other martial arts and not deviate even a little

from the Way of the warrior. With your spirit settled, accumulate practice day by day, and hour by hour. Polish the twofold spirit, heart and mind, and sharpen the twofold gaze, perception and sight. When your spirit is not in the least clouded, when the clouds of bewilderment clear away, there is the true void.

Until you realize the true Way, whether in Buddhism or in common sense, you may think that things are correct and in order. However, if we look at things objectively, from the viewpoint of laws of the world, we see various doctrines departing from the true Way. Know well this spirit, and with forthrightness as the foundation and the true spirit as the Way. Enact strategy broadly, correctly and openly.

Then you will come to think of things in a wide sense and, taking the void as the Way, you will see the Way as void.

In the void is virtue, and no evil. Wisdom has existence, principle has existence, the Way has existence, spirit is nothingness.

ENLIGHTENMENT

M usashi's fifth and final book is 'The Void'.
It is short and appears at first read to be a complete departure from the four books that precede it. However, this fifth and final ring is the sum total of the other four rings; the perfect end game that constitutes the enlightened condition one can and should attain if Musashi's messages have been absorbed and applied. 'By knowing things that exist, you can know that which does not exist. That is the void,' he says.

The state of emptiness 'The Book of the Void' speaks to is not about being vacuous or inert; rather, so calm and clear of distraction that one is hyper-sensitive to all prevailing forces and dynamics. Ignorance may be bliss and the ignorant pure, but such individuals will never come close to the void. 'People in this world look at things mistakenly, and think that what

they do not understand must be the void. This is not the true void. It is bewilderment,' says Musashi.

Being all-seeing and all-knowing is quite a claim to make for oneself, but Musashi seems to do so by suggesting that true illumination awaits those that follow his instruction. For he starts the book by saying, 'The *Nito Ichi* Way of strategy is recorded in this, the "Book of the Void".'

He goes on to note that when one realizes 'the true Way ... Then you will come to think of things in a wide sense and, taking the void as the Way, you will see the Way as void.' Ergo, he considers the Way and the void to be one and the same, and an understanding of the void to be the ultimate edification and release from earthly matters. 'By knowing things that exist, you can know that which does not exist. That is the void.'

In truth, Musashi had more of a claim than most to be infinite, having never lost a duel and having spent a lifetime in dedication to self-improvement.

No Short Cuts

There are no short cuts to this promised land for the warrior. Only by devoting themselves to training in the Way Musashi has outlined across *The Book of Five Rings* can the necessary conditions be created for the mists to clear and access be afforded to this higher realm. 'When your spirit is not in the least clouded, when the clouds of bewilderment clear away, there is the true void,' he explains.

The same is true for the entrepreneur. Illumination cannot be acquired transactionally. One cannot hustle one's way to

it, and it will elude the impatient or the demanding. Entrance to the abstract void is marked by a very high bar that exists peripherally. Paradoxically, if we think we're so together we've cleared that bar, this strongly indicates we haven't, since this betrays inadequate humility. It also speaks to a mistaken belief that the void is a definable realm one could ever be capable of proving one was present in.

If this all sounds a bit infuriating, that is just the point. Because only by letting go and relinquishing the worldly need to exercise control can a person surrender enough of themselves to be admitted entry. For a contemporary manifestation of Musashi's meaning, think of the wise Jedi master Obi-Wan Kenobi in *Star Wars* attempting to school young Luke Skywalker in the ways of the universe. 'Use the force Luke, let go,' he entreated him.

Musashi wrote *The Book of Five Rings* in his twilight years, and he could only have concluded it in the way he did with 'The Book of the Void' on the back of having lived a full life. With this final thoughtful flourish, while ostensibly instructing the reader, what we are witnessing is Musashi reflecting on his accumulated wisdom and seeking to attach some palpable worth to it. In doing so, he takes a qualitative, rather than quantitative approach and describes the reward for following his teachings as so profound it is intangible.

As a blueprint for how to conduct oneself and get on in modern business, 'The Book of the Void' – despite being just a few paragraphs long – packs a lot of punch with its pithy proclamations.

Timeless Truths

'Enact strategy broadly, correctly and openly,' is a key phrase. It speaks to a core Musashi theme that can be readily supplanted to present-time entrepreneurial proceedings.

Just like 'transparency', 'accountability' and 'responsibility' are the watchwords of today's corporate arena, woe betide the entrepreneur that doesn't get on board with such notions. Nor is it enough to simply pay lip service to progressiveness and leading by example, for newly empowered stakeholders take a dim view of hypocrisy and counterfeit credentials.

So, whether you're yet to embark on your business journey, currently accelerating, or established and looking to consolidate, it is expected of every company and its representatives these days that they mean what they say, that what they say expresses clear values, and that actions match words.

Broadly

'Enact strategy broadly,' says Musashi.

This does not mean attempting to be all things to all people. Instead, it is about taking a 'big picture', holistic approach and being cognisant of the potential for a curveball of any description to come one's way from any direction.

'Broadly' means being inclusive; where one stands for something, yet all are welcome. Not all the invited will beat a path to one's door, for unless one has a monopoly on air, shelter, food or water, the appeal of anything else is down to taste and preference. But in positioning as a church where

all are welcome, one's product or service – and by extension oneself – will have managed to successfully prove that, paradoxically, one can have a strong tribal identity and at the same time be accommodative to people and ideas. Always open, always learning, just as Musashi would advocate. This will inexorably garner the respect even of those for whom what is on offer is not their thing. This represents healthy competition and is what today's entrepreneur should aspire towards.

Today, many businesses large and small claim to put corporate social responsibility, diversity and inclusivity at the heart of what they do. In reality, the majority of efforts could best be described as high-profile overtures or grandiose gestures designed to appease evolving consumer expectations. They should be considered more as a clinical response to market surveys and focus groups related to reputation management and corporate governance than evidence of a seismic shift in strategic thinking that places people and planet over – or at least alongside – profits.

Not all such moves are inauthentic. Certainly, many entrepreneurs would like to do more, yet fear that being green and sustainable are anathema to free market thinking and will disadvantage their business in relation to competitors who show no inclination to change. After all, to enact strategy broadly is going to cost, right? So, while it's good to do the right thing, it's not so nice if it means the business goes under.

In truth, the market has developed a conscience it did not previously possess. The accumulated ravages wrought by

endless inequality and unchecked capitalism mean more and more people are fed up with the status quo from which so few benefit. And, in the developed world at least, new thinking has succeeded the traditionally understood end game state of high mass consumption, with raw economics being fused with social and environmental considerations that attach value to people and the planet we live on. This has found expression in notions such as natural capital, ethical investing and diversity quotas.

As ever, actions speak louder than words, but there are a growing number of companies proving that there is nothing incompatible between being tangibly empathetic and profitable.

Elon Musk's Tesla company shows that the manufacture of environmentally friendlier electric vehicles to supersede their high-emission gas-guzzling predecessors can be applied at scale. This has allowed the firm to become one of the leading electric vehicle (EV) manufacturers worldwide with a market capitalization of over $800 billion, while at the same time showing we can all keep on the move without destroying the planet.

Musk's broad strategic actions are helping to consign the internal combustion engine to history, which will go some way to ameliorating humanity's existential prospects. In the process Tesla – just one in his portfolio of companies that also includes the social media application X (formerly Twitter) and SpaceX – employs 127,000 workers across the world, with governments competing to woo the world's

richest man to set up his latest manufacturing facility in their backyard. Musk appears keen on a meritocracy that has hard work as its defining criteria and seeks to be inclusive to the point of letting anyone and everyone have a platform. As to the appropriateness or otherwise of his approach to freedom of speech, that is a separate debate. But as a successful manifestation of the broad church theory, Elon Musk is the ultimate example and proof of how apt Musashi's words are today.

Correctly

'Enact strategy ... correctly,' declares Musashi.

It is not enough these days for a business to focus exclusively on the bottom line or to use profit seeking as the end that justifies the means. Rather, today's Mr or Mrs Corporate needs to be sensitive to the shifting sands of convention, and also be alert to societal developments taking place at a distance.

Events may appear to be happening elsewhere with little capacity to impact one's fortunes, and company results may indicate one is successfully speaking the language of one's target market. However, being ignorant of or uninterested in the evolving consensus beyond what is immediately visible can lead to one becoming significantly out of step with current thinking. This is why Musashi directs us to 'sharpen the twofold gaze, perception and sight'. Failure to do so can lead one to being 'cancelled'.

Although theoretically afforded the right of reply when an unfavourable narrative takes hold, turning the weight and

tide of negative public opinion once it has gained traction is nigh on impossible. Like rats leaving a sinking ship, those stakeholders formerly aligned to one's business, brand and cause will vanish once they perceive they have become lodged in a space on the wrong side of the argument.

Entrepreneurs must always have in mind that there is no loyalty on the business battleground. People are drawn to winners and what associating with success might bring their way in the form of connections and material enhancement. Equally, they will desert a loser at the drop of a hat, since there's neither stardust nor money in siding with unpopular people or organizations.

Self-made and mega-successful *Harry Potter* author J. K. Rowling knows exactly how difficult it can be to win back trust once lost. After making what some consider were transphobic comments the writer was criticized and her work and its franchise boycotted by elements of her huge fanbase.

From the late 2010s, the career, lucrative sponsorship deals and product tie-ins of recording artist Kanye West took a huge hit when he seemingly positioned himself in direct opposition to movements such as Black Lives Matter and #MeToo, while at the same time appearing to espouse antisemitic beliefs.

Openly

'Enact strategy … openly,' decrees Musashi.

When one is honest, straightforward, scrupulous and ethical in one's dealings, it limits the ability of others to

manipulate a situation or to create a false narrative that would act against one's interests. While this will not eliminate completely the scope for antagonistic forces to wield the malicious axe, being able to evidence integrity will afford one a measure of protection.

However, with the proliferation of platforms where companies are now expected to have a presence, and where those with a clear and distinct voice get noticed, a high multi-channel profile underpinned by regular, active and resonant messaging can massively boost one's fortunes. However, if even one of those messages is deemed too controversial by a critical mass with the platform, it can spell trouble. The moral of the story here is that one can enact strategy too 'openly'. Being wholly true to oneself publicly as well as privately is naïve. Keeping a little back until one gauges the lay of the land is not being insincere or duplicitous – it is just common sense.

Nor does it have to mean that one becomes lost in the crowd. It is expected of the modern business leader that they are sensitive, inclusive and compassionate. Part of the art of making commercial headway lies in accepting that any enterprise can, in its messaging and communication, unintentionally cause offence – and react in a way that tries to avoid causing further offence while staying true to one's core values.

This does not mean one's rhetoric has to be ubiquitous, forgettable or overworked. It simply acknowledges that there are red lines. When a company's fortunes take a downturn, it is often the case that nothing has materially altered, but

that an opposing force has found an opening for advantage through a red line having been crossed and has run with it. By not gifting the competition an advantage through loose talk or reckless actions, an entrepreneur will be more likely to ensure the continued success of their company.

In the case of Chinese multinational tech firm, Alibaba, its founder Jack Ma, a former English teacher and China's wealthiest person, fell foul of his country's rulers when he made a controversial speech in 2020 that criticized China's financial regulators for their risk-averse approach to commerce. The nation's leaders decided that Ma was too outspoken and wielded too much power and influence, and he mysteriously disappeared from view for three months. When he resurfaced in January 2021, Ma was no longer China's dominant entrepreneur. A regulatory clampdown had diminished the size and profitability of his businesses and he had effectively been removed from front-line commerce.

Respect the Sequence

'The Book of the Void' is about reaching that place where one can operate instinctively. But the precursor to being intuitive is that one must strive for a lifetime marked by meticulousness, studiousness and purposefulness. For Musashi, this evolutionary sequence is inviolable, unalterable and constitutes the natural order of things. Enlightenment doesn't just happen; it is the reward for a lifetime of sacrifice, humility and dedication. Those upstart over-confident entrepreneurs that think they know everything, perhaps

buoyed by early good fortune, will soon become unstuck when the luck they mistakenly identified as skill runs out.

It was just the same for the samurai warriors of yesteryear, who would often have a higher opinion of themselves than was warranted and only came to realize they were not as good as they thought they were when it was too late to do anything about it in a sometimes fatal moment of epiphany.

For the entrepreneur, while lives are unlikely to be immediately at risk from failure, livelihoods are. The reputational damage can be very real and long lasting too, along with the hit to one's confidence. Confidence and optimism are essential qualities to cultivate and are exhibited by the most successful entrepreneurs. Arrogance and recklessness are their bad relations, and they lurk nearby. Be careful not to invite them in.

Musashi's Legacy

Ethereal, abstract and insubstantial, 'The Book of the Void' ultimately speaks to the illusory nature of worldly things. Already into his seventh decade when he penned *The Book of Five Rings* – a ripe old age in the seventeenth century – Musashi would have known his time on Earth was drawing to a close. In looking back at his life and work through an autobiographical lens, he was subconsciously elevating in meaning the death that was irresistibly coming his way. To understand and temper the enormity of what he must have known was just around the corner, it made sense for him to cast his life as simply the preliminary stage to the main event.

Entrepreneurs – especially those champing at the bit to get started – should exercise a degree of caution when onboarding his thinking. Note well that the state of transcendence he advocates striving for in 'The Book of the Void' is not one likely to resonate with venture capitalists, angel investors, seed funds or business incubators, who are likely to mistake this state of being for an unattractive mixture of hubris and lethargy.

And despite his obvious successes in the duelling arena, here was a man interested in his legacy. That he set this out in *The Book of Five Rings* means we must take time to question the sentiments contained within, recognizing that they are intended to portray the correct and logical conclusions to the journey of life that he writes about.

In this way, all points on that journey will be painted in a favourable light and seen as essential touchpoints in informing the ultimate finished product – namely, himself. Musashi's starting point appears to be that he is occupying the state of nirvana that all should hope to achieve, and, therefore, that everything he did up to that point is unarguably correct and is what everyone should seek to emulate. This smacks of confirmation bias.

The point here is that we only see what Musashi wants us to see. Broadly speaking, it's hard to argue with his 'true Way', but when it comes to specifics we must each forge our own path. What works for one entrepreneur is unlikely to work for another, since the forces at play and the cast of actors are different.

CONCLUSION

It is noteworthy that *The Book of Five Rings* commences with 'The Book of the Ground' and then moves through the ever more intangible, immaterial elements of water, fire and wind to the ultimate state of emptiness represented by the void. It is the truest and worthiest of journeys Musashi asks us to join him on, where he divests himself of earthly pleasures and preoccupations, transcending the material boundaries of body, mind and soul to become at one with the universe.

Giving such outwardly wispy sentiments credence sounds very new age, but in brushing aside such notions for fear of being considered unbusiness-like, we ignore the large appetite in corporate circles today for the east-west fusion approach to business and personal growth.

The Stanford Graduate School of Business (GSB) in California is a veritable breeding ground for entrepreneurs.

It can boast among its alumni figures such as Nike co-founder and chairman emeritus, Phil Knight, pioneer of discounted sales of equity securities, Charles Schwab, and co-founder of Sun Microsystems, Vinod Khosla. This venerable institution, which churns out free-thinking movers and shakers as if they're coming off a production line, offers students a programme on interpersonal dynamics, colloquially known as the 'Touchy-Feely' course. Designed to help would-be entrepreneurs unlock their true leadership potential, it has been consistently voted the most popular GSB elective for almost half a century.

With many of today's most influential global entrepreneurs having taken an expansive approach to life from an early age, it would seem that those with a predisposition towards blended body and soul are disproportionately adept at outpacing the competition. And, having reached the lofty heights of commerce, are equally adroit at staying there.

Steve Jobs, Richard Branson, and Ben Cohen and Jerry Greenfield of Ben & Jerry's fame are but four examples that lend weight to the theory one can be both a hippy and a capitalist. Some would say the ruthlessness such individuals have shown in getting to the top and maintaining that elevated status renders them conservatives masquerading as progressives. However, Musashi shows us that being in a state of equilibrium with oneself and one's surroundings is fully compatible with success that – by the normal commercial measuring mechanisms – records one as having performed better than one's peers.

Ironically, it is rarely the billionaire entrepreneurs themselves who wish to advertise their net worth or consider it to be a relevant marker of their value or achievements. That is the preserve of those on the outside looking in, usually the type to criticize rather than critique, and often green with envy towards those higher up the pecking order than themselves.

Of course, the avaricious and the vauntful exist, and there are also those that have done nothing to earn their fame or fortune. And everyone could no doubt do more to achieve more in life. However, for most business icons it is the chance to make a difference to other people's lives and society that primarily drives them, and to deliver on that objective requires one's commercial interests to do well.

There are only so many houses, yachts or private islands one can own before a saturation point of enjoyment is reached. Thereafter, for the contemplative person, it soon becomes apparent that quality of life is to be found in the same places that it existed before the riches arrived. If one loved solving problems before, for example, they will still enjoy it now.

'Exist for the good of Man,' says Master Musashi. He also instructs the reader not to 'seek pleasure for its own sake'.

Those that pursue a life of self-indulgence once success has been attained betray a decided lack of imagination, and while they may have money, they are poor where it really counts. They may continue to be acclaimed and celebrated as successful businesspeople, but they are not entrepreneurs, because the true entrepreneur cannot resist the next great

enterprise. They remain fundamentally go-getting, yet humble enough to keep learning, no matter how successful they become.

'Carry no money or food. Go alone to places frightening to the common brand of men. Become a criminal of purpose. Be put in jail, and extricate yourself by your own wisdom.' Musashi knew the path to enlightenment was unpaved and must be walked alone, demanding that one renounce pleasure for purpose. In business, if that purpose is only to enrich oneself at the expense of others, then the product or service one is pushing will inevitably become disengaged from its target market.

Consumers want to be aligned with a company's values that reflect their own. If they feel there is a values vacuum at the heart of an organization, they will consider this – often instinctively – reason enough to end the relationship. Equally, if the message coming out of the company that is seeking to appeal can be scrutinized and is auditable, that will chime more than one that simply says the right things.

This was the case with Anita Roddick and continues to inform the Body Shop brand she founded. Alongside no animal testing, and the promotion of a fairer deal for farmers and suppliers, the company has always sought to place female empowerment at the heart of its identity and values since it first opened its doors in 1976. From that moment, it has always endeavoured to align with its founding principle that business is a force for good. It was the Body Shop's radically different approach to commerce from the established beauty

industry players that drove its growth, spearheaded by Roddick's convictions and her commitment to the cause.

Like Musashi, such folk may like to confidently wax lyrical regarding the efficacy of their Way, but this should not be seen as showmanship. Rather, like Musashi, they really believe in what they are saying and want to share this enlightenment with others.

To the Nerd Go the Spoils

Many of the most successful entrepreneurs today either consider themselves to be or have been diagnosed as being what's informally known as 'on the spectrum', whereby their brain works in a different way to the majority of the population.

No doubt the entrepreneurial ranks were always jam-packed with high functioning autistics, those with attention deficit hyperactivity disorder (ADHD), individuals who would today be diagnosed with Asperger's Syndrome, or considered neurodiverse, but for whom such diagnoses or descriptions had yet to emerge.

Zuckerberg, Branson, Musk, Bezos, Schwab, Jobs and Gates are all part of this club. In other words, the world's most successful entrepreneurs have not been held back by their Musashi-like intensity and insistence on doing things differently, because they recognize that this constitutes a better way than what preceded it. Indeed, such 'conditions' have actively advantaged them. Their apparent dysfunction, which causes them to view the world through

a nonconformist lens, also allows them to see pathways and resolutions obscured to others imprisoned by convention. Musashi says that 'Men must polish their own way,' and tells us to 'Think lightly of yourself and deeply of the world.'

These entrepreneurs have no need to polish, since to them their reasoned Way is the only Way. And despite the cultural conditioning that says such individuals are egocentric, their sense of self is, conversely, usually underdeveloped. What may appear to be self-absorption to others is often simply the entrepreneur's analysis of the closest and most convenient object for study, and the only one they have direct experiential insight into: themselves. Just like Musashi, such individuals tend to be able to multitask, bring consistently high levels of energy to the table and switch tasks swiftly and easily.

Relatable they may not be, but pure and authentic they are. In truth, they wouldn't know how or why to be anything other than themselves, and their natural focus on objectivity acts to cut through the infinite layers of nonsense that traditionally cloak the marketplace.

Perfection is an Illusion. Strive for Best Possible

Musashi's ambition for both himself and others could best be described as soaring. His entreaties that beseech us to heed his warnings are nothing if not well intentioned. But while he looks to create the conditions in us that mean we will not bow to convention, in its place he risks putting something equally prescriptive.

Being a business leader can be a lonely endeavour, and while Musashi provides some comfort blanket truths to cling on to when we're fumbling in the dark for the light switch or the path becomes obscured, the most successful entrepreneurs ultimately are unique and must trust in their own customized truths, regardless of the resistance from naysayers and doubters. As Albert Einstein wrote in 1940: 'Great spirits have always encountered violent opposition from mediocre minds.'

For those entrepreneurs spending borrowed money, which is most of them, time tends not to be on their side. Investors want to see a return on their investment – often sooner rather than later – and so the strategy one deploys to meet this priority requirement can be at odds with the concept of there being a right time for everything. Sometimes, one is compelled to take action now that would ideally have happened at a later date.

While Musashi speaks much to the importance of timing, so too does he promote a perspective that balances immediate metrics with long-term goals. Sometimes, there is no time to find a vantage point that affords a 360° view of one's surroundings, and short-term survival mode takes over instead. The ability to find a way through by applying the appropriate tactics to prevail at such moments does not have to be inconsistent with the overall strategic vision, however, and is as essential to the entrepreneurs' makeup as it was to the samurai warriors' composition.

Musashi might also point out that any remuneration agreement with investors, whether centred upon regular instalments, equity or a straight repayment, should not be so disadvantageous to the entrepreneur that it becomes a challenge to fulfil. If that turns out to be the case, one must reflect on why it was entered into in the first place. The investee will presumably have signed any such agreement in good faith, so that the extent and nature of their commitments should have been clear in advance of the event. Failure to acknowledge or prepare for what was on the horizon shows a lack of perception and sight, as Musashi would have it, and indicates that more and better training is needed.

That said, *The Book of Five Rings* was written by a man who seemingly never tasted nor was chastened by the bitter tang of defeat. So, while we can applaud the intent of his instruction to be like him and never lose, his words can sound a little unforgiving for the many that will encounter failure on their journey. To appear to exclude such enterprising folk for faltering, despite Musashi implicitly acknowledging one will always be a work in progress, and therefore, by extension, fallible, does his message a disservice. And so, in today's less rigid world we may take his absolutes with a pinch of salt.

We Think, Therefore We Succeed

Musashi's self-help bible is marked by being accessible and comprehensible to all, just like all the best works that come to endure and transcend cultural boundaries.

That is not to say it is an everyman tome. While its language can be understood by everyone, its themes are likely to resonate deeply only with certain Myers Briggs personality types: namely, the ENTP, ESTJ, ENTJ and INTJ types, where 'E' stands for 'Extroverted', 'N' for 'iNtuitive', 'T' for 'Thinking', 'P' for Perceiving', 'S' for 'Sensing', 'J' for 'Judging', and 'I' for 'Introversion'.

Most entrepreneurs fall into one of these four personality types from the pool of 16 possibilities, with the common characteristic this quartet shares being 'Thinking', suggesting the key to successful entrepreneurialism is to be a critical thinker. This is borne out by entrepreneurs' use of facts, data, logic and objectivity as they look to identify obstacles, solve problems and determine the optimum way forward.

This sits in alignment with Musashi's Way that has no place for emotion-driven decision-making or stab-in-the-dark guesswork.

Commentator, comedian, actor and martial arts aficionado Joe Rogan has sported a tattoo of Miyamoto Musashi on his right arm since the age of 16. When talking on his podcast of his admiration for the messages contained within *The Book of Five Rings* he draws his listeners' attention to the passage, 'If you know the Way broadly, you will see it in everything.'

Rogan urges his audience to apply Musashi's teaching, believing that once one dedicates oneself to improving in respect of a particular discipline, this can then be applied to any number of other things to enhance one's existence. For him, Musashi's text is the blueprint to becoming a

Renaissance man. He explains that, 'Difficult things are tools to maximize the way your mind interacts with life.'

Rogan's is perhaps the most high-profile endorsement of Musashi's pearls of wisdom, for other celebrities wanting to promote their Zen credentials and be seen as well-read and erudite tend to align themselves with more high profile eastern philosophical texts, such as Lao Tzu's *Tao Te Ching*, *The Analects* by Confucius, Fu Xi's *The I Ching*, or, more recently, *The Way of Zen* by Alan Watts, which helped to introduce and popularize eastern philosophy for a Western audience hitherto mostly unaware of its reverberant qualities.

As important and eye-opening as such books are, *The Book of Five Rings* is distinct in focusing on the individual condition and journey. As such, it is perfect for the lone-ranging entrepreneur confronted by and in need of a fundamental source mechanism to cope with and overcome myriad unprovoked challenges. It is as much for the present-day minnows dreaming of becoming big fish as it is for those already wielding authority and commanding attention who wish to keep it that way.

Inferred Enlightenment

One of the key takeaways from *The Book of Five Rings* is that knowledge does not have to be represented or proven to be considered real.

The sceptical might say this is the usual get around from those with faith, and that Musashi's winning ways and the successes enjoyed by his army of disciples looking to

implement his teachings are the consequence of a placebo effect unleashed at scale.

However, those entrepreneurs struggling to look at life through an Eastern lens might like to consider Musashi's recorded triumphs as the reflection of the enlightened state of being he had reached. It is rather like inferring what a distant galaxy looked like millions of years ago from the state of a beam of light today.

Musashi identified having a strategy (and the right strategy at that) as the key to winning any contest. His perfect duelling record is all the evidence we need that he got it right.

Entrepreneurs act on the back of the best possible information available in the requisite time frame, while others theorize and remain inert, rendered incapable of action through analysis paralysis and the fear of getting it wrong. They console themselves that anything and everything remains possible while no action is taken, and that way failure is kept at bay. The entrepreneur recognizes how ludicrous such inertia is and is interested only in the strategy that is both implementable and implemented. Unless one gets to put a strategy into practice, how can one know one has got it right?

As the British wartime Prime Minister Winston Churchill once said: 'However beautiful the strategy, you should occasionally look at the results.'

The Truth is Out There

Musashi believes strongly in the power of acceptance. He advocates living in the present without regret, expectation

or judgement, and not raging over things one has no control over. To do otherwise is to become distracted. 'Accept everything just the way it is,' he says.

Importantly, this does not mean being passive. One must still act – and act assertively – to get things done, but those actions should always be informed by reality rather than an imagined world of self-delusion. And while bad actors such as narcissists can exploit reality for advantage by dividing and ruling and peddling untruths, these tactics will only ever provide enough sustenance for low-level enterprise. Despite their raging ambition and boundless motivation, the self-serving bias such individuals are prone to means they are incapable of learning and growing, since they cannot admit to any shortcomings that would necessitate change. This means their entrepreneurial endeavours will forever at best be stuck on a cycle of repeat. The true entrepreneur always wants to end each day a better person than they started it and recognizes that the only way they can do that is to embrace the truth.

The last word must of course go to Master Musashi who reminds us that, 'Truth is not what you want it to be; it is what it is. And you must bend to its power or live a lie.'

INDEX